Contents

To Siri, James and Rebecca

The Youth Training Scheme:
A New Curriculum

23.

3(

The Youth Training Scheme: Scheme: A New Curriculum?

EPISODE 1

Terry Edwards

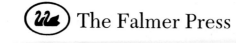 The Falmer Press

A member of the Taylor & Francis Group
London and Philadelphia

UK   The Falmer Press, Falmer House, Barcombe, Lewes, East Sussex, BN8 5DL

USA   The Falmer Press, Taylor & Francis Inc., 242 Cherry Street, Philadelphia, PA 19106-1906

First published in 1984

Library of Congress Cataloging in Publication Data

Edwards, Terry.
   The youth training scheme—a new curriculum?

   Bibliography: p.
   Includes indexes.
   1. Education, Secondary—Great Britain—Curricula.
2. Curriculum change—Great Britain. 3. Youth—
Employment—Great Britain. I. Title.
LB1629.5.G7E39 1983 375′.00941 83-25380
ISBN 0-905273-96-6
ISBN 0-905273-95-8 (pbk.)

Typeset in 11/13 Bembo
by Imago Publishing, Thame, Oxon.

Jacket design by Leonard Williams

Printed in Great Britain by Taylor & Francis (Printers) Ltd, Basingstoke

List of Figures and Tables

Preface

The viewpoint of this book can be likened to that of the spectator on the sidelines of a game being played by an indeterminate number of sides of various and changeable compositions, refereed by several obscure figures, some of whom seem more important than others, and whose affiliations seem less than neutral. Adding to the (fatal) fascination of this game is the curious, but distinct impression that several teams seem to be winning, and that there is a surprising, but suspiciously false, consensus about this. No one seems to mind about the various industrious groundsmen who move goal posts from place to place unless their particular posts seem to be the object of attention.

Most of the participants, including the referees and groundsmen, seem to agree the game is worthwhile, and seem to tacitly recognize the various goals in the game. Indeed, there is an odd convention that there is only one goal without exact agreement as to its location. Scoring appears to depend on nods and winks from whichever referee will oblige.

Outside the stadium queues are thought to be forming. The present spectator is intensely curious to know what the queues of young people are going to do when they are let in to have a go at getting a goal, whether their goals will count, whether they can score at all, and whether the game will do them any good once they leave the stadium.

This spectator, in the shape of the author, is distinctly ambivalent about the whole thing, but cannot help watching and wondering if it will come to something for all concerned or not. The author is also sensitive to the fact that new players, rules, referees and sundry other paraphernalia are sure to appear the minute pen is taken from paper and laid to rest. Perhaps, readers will bear in mind that *episode one* did end rather arbitrarily in March 1983.

1 Curriculum: The One Thing Needful

The point is, could many people with the right educational help, achieve still more? ... the future pattern of employment in this country will require a much larger pool of talent than is at present available; and that at least a substantial proportion of the 'average' and 'below average' pupils are sufficiently educable to supply that additional talent. The need is not only for more skilled workers to fill existing jobs, but also for a generally better educated and intelligently adaptable labour force to meet new demands...

Newsom Report (1963) *Half Our Future*, report of the Minister of Education's Central Advisory Council

A sense of *déjà vu* permeates this book. The 'half' talked about herein is still largely the Newsom (1963) half, and talked about in terms of giving them a suitable, worthwhile, relevant curriculum. The talk, the debate, and the 'scheming' which seems to be following, is presently centred on what to do with, for, or to, 16–19-year-olds who are unemployed. Inextricably entangled with this curricular scheming is the question of what to do about examining 16-year-olds and the concomitant (or is it the other way round?) hand-wringing about the pre-16 secondary school curriculum. The train-'em versus the educate-'em brigades mutter darkly about demarcation and speculate about new distinctions, needs, and definitions of what they mean.

Unemployment is now a major feature in the old bottom half syndrome. Agendas for action are redolent with Newsom language: 'patterns of employment', 'relevance', 'below average', 'new skills', 'intelligence' and 'adaptability', 'world of work', 'real world', 'industry', and so on. Conventional wisdom is that 16–19-year-olds need training for jobs, and jobs seem collectively synonymous with industry; but 'there are no jobs' is the somewhat sweeping statement bandied around by cynics, politicians and arguers in general. Yet, getting jobs still seems vital, education seems to have failed in giving leavers such skills. It's education's fault. It?

What is *it*? On the one hand it is unemployment, on the other it is the normal desire of the 16-year-old leaver to live conventionally in a society which values work very highly in social terms, if not always in economic terms. To live conventionally the 16-year-old leaver must get a job, and this means paid employment. To live conventionally the 16-year-old leaver needs an income. But the structure of work is changing and the nature of labour market demand is changing. *It* is certainly changing, both in kind and, temporarily it is hoped, in quantity. Education's fault, presumably, is to do with not keeping up with such changes, and indeed not being right in the first place. Education, it is suspected, has not been, and is not, doing the right things to/for young people. Their needs and 'industry's' needs seem synonymous when they often do in fact need, desperately, a job. In the present climate of widespread and increasing unemployment, conflation of the needs of industry with the needs of young people is persuasive and commonplace among ordinary people; although many recognize the obvious contradiction, and supplement the conflation with 'what's the point, anyway, if there are no jobs'. But 'something' must be done.

Doing 'something' is a political necessity, even if education can mysteriously take some of the blame for young people not getting jobs. If the 'something' can also act as an instrument of educational policy, then the 'something' is certainly politically attractive. If the idea of a comprehensive education for all can be re-attached to the needs of industry being synonymous with the needs of the individual, then it is a short step to conflating training (that is, really useful knowledge) with education, and an even shorter step after that to separating the sheep from the goats, and ensuring they graze the appropriate curricula. As everyone, in the last analysis, needs to eat, then curricula will be grazed, tastes acquired and futures ordained. If doing 'something' creates a curriculum for the bottom half which satisfies their need to eat, and even takes care to check their digestion, then *the* curriculum of upward mobility (for the goats?) can be reserved as fodder for the bright and/or the privileged. But if the two curricula are in practice insulated from each other, then what? – then what indeed? At this time 'something' is wrapped up in the schemes of the Manpower Services

Commission (MSC); that the future of the secondary school curriculum is also under these wraps is perhaps obvious. At its simplest, what is happening, in effect, is the formalization, documentation and 'improvement' of that 'other' (informal) secondary school curriculum for the less bright, as the other half are commonly described. What is involved is the development of a 'new curriculum' in the guise of MSC schemes relevant for and to the less bright, which will ensure they have the skills and inclination to work, when work is available. What these skills are and how they are best learnt, and how inclination to work is maintained or induced, is the subject of the present debate about schemes for the young unemployed.

What is now very clear indeed is that the whole secondary school curriculum has been put on the operating table by the present government. The intention is to manoeuvre consensual views about the necessity for change so as to remould the educational system along conservative ideological lines. The debate and the decisions on schemes for 16–17-year-old unemployed have been leading to the formation and practice of a new curriculum. The centre of the debate has been and continues to be curricula and their relevance.

The New Training Initiative Youth Training Scheme (YTS) has been presented to the country in terms of a training programme apparently related to the needs of young people leaving school, namely, to be adequately prepared to do work if and when it is available. The scheme is apparently a training programme within industry, funded and controlled by the MSC, and partly serviced on a fee contract basis by the Further Education Service, although LEAs and some individual FE institutions have attempted to become full provider organizations in their own right. In many cases substantial experience with the predecessor Youth Opportunities Scheme (YOP) has created an expectation that the new YTS scheme is mainly a curriculum innovation/development, an extension and improvement on the YOP. In such cases there has often been a failure to recognize the deeper political significance of the introduction of YTS. Of course, there is general recognition that YTS means change, but its potential as a wedge placed in the rapidly extending split in the present secondary school curriculum has barely been appreciated. A few blows from such financial heavyweights as the New Training and Vocational Education Initiative (NTVEI) will certainly ensure the old divide between technical secondary modern and grammar school opens up again, at least in curricular terms (initially), rather than through any overt institutional appearance.

Because curriculum is of such central importance, the word is used throughout this book. Consequently, the meaning it is given, or takes on, is crucial. This first chapter is an attempt to develop a new definition of curriculum to enable, in particular, the 'new curriculum' to be more adequately and precisely analyzed in terms of its practical effects upon participants. As will become clearer, curriculum participants are those individuals and groups who are *members* of a curriculum organization. A curriculum is identified less in terms of what is to be learnt (syllabus) than in terms of it being, de facto, an organization with members. It is admitted immediately that this is a somewhat tentative concept, and that it is not the purpose of this book to establish it in any full or final sense. Considerable exploration of the state of organization theory linked to substantial curricular research would be an undoubted requirement for a substantiation of the concept of curriculum as organization. Nevertheless, the attempt is made to describe, analyze and discuss the YTS proposals in terms of this tentative concept of curriculum. The main object of this book is therefore to describe, analyze and discuss the 'new curriculum' and, indeed, to identify it as a curriculum of revolutionary, or more accurately, counter-revolutionary significance. But, because the word 'curriculum' is itself at the heart of the book, and is used in such a newly developed, if tentative way, it is necessary to clarify what is meant by curriculum, or *a* curriculum, or *the* curriculum.

Any study of education reveals immediately the extraordinary ubiquity of the word, and not only its ubiquity but its ambiguity. Such revelation is, of course, commonplace, nevertheless it is, perhaps, the only truly unambiguous point of departure. Attempting to give the word,

> '. . . some formal definition does not begin to suggest the scope of what falls under the rubric 'curriculum' when words such as construction, planning, or development are added to it. For example, curriculum development can mean the careful arranging of step-by-step 'sets' in a planned sequence designed to produce a reading skill in pupils. Equally legitimately, it means the total array of efforts of a nation to develop programs of study for students at elementary, secondary, and tertiary levels of the formal educational system. And this, in turn, can include both the sociopolitical processes involved and the fruits emanating from them in the form of intended learnings for students. The study of curriculum might and does include activities at the former, specific level and at the latter, broad or general level, and a great deal in between. (Goodlad *et al.*, 1979, p. 44)

However, when a definition is (by definition) required, the *Shorter Oxford English Dictionary* (3rd ed., rev., 1956) provides an interestingly curt response: 'Curriculum: A course; *spec* a regular course of study as at a school or (Scottish) university.' This is, at first sight, reassuring, until the possibilities of the word 'course' are examined. With this the matter is returned to Goodlad's 1979 putative distinction between specific experience constructs for intended learnings, and the broad *effect* of an array of organized or constructed learning experiences in society. These are part of a continuum of social behaviour and not a series, or sequence, of insulated actions. This is to include, therefore, the important notion that a planned, specific, sequence of intended learnings necessarily incorporates the experiences inherent in the broader socio-political context within which they occur. Of course, this may be extending the effect too far toward the indiscernible, or rather the indecipherable, regions of sociological process; this is to say, indecipherable to students and teachers actually caught up in that flux of interactions wherein 'organized learning' occurs. A curriculum in this sense is no more discontinuous with its socio-political environment than any other human organization in society.

The idea, then, of curriculum as a course of study is of little direct use. Nevertheless, the notion of 'regularity' about a course of study is helpful. It is helpful in the respect that it identifies a difference between experience per se, and experience which is organized, which has a deliberative internal logic regulating it, or attempting to. Failure to entirely regulate the experience of other human beings is fortunately inevitable. Consequently, a course of study always involves more than its internal logic. At the least it must include not only its organized content, but also its method. What is experienced is both the content and the method of teaching.

> Properly understood, the concept of the curriculum involves far more than the content of education: it is not to be identified with subject-matter or with syllabuses and schemes of work. How we teach is as much a part of it as what we teach. Curricular problems, in other words, cannot be dissociated from problems of methodology. (Richmond, 1968, p. 194)

While it can be, and perhaps should be, argued that the identification and organization of the internal logic of a course of studies is of considerable pedagogical value, it should not be overlooked that there is both the 'logic' of the subject to be learned and the logic of how best its 'logic' should be learned. Attempts to create theories of instruction (for example, Bruner, 1966) are attempts to further this distinction and construct a practice upon it.

A deeper, and indeed immensely more intricate, development is most notably that of Bloom and colleagues (1956, 1964). Bloom's taxonomy of educational objectives is entirely useful at its basic conceptual level, but subject to the most tortuous, and finally indecipherable practice, collapsing under the weight of its own distinctions. There is a certain, if peculiar, justice in:

> They [Bloom *et al*] found it easy enough to show that one could construct a taxonomy of mental skills in which each level was included in and subordinated by the next so that knowledge of trivial facts was both clearly inferior to and yet necessary to higher levels of understanding. Their ideological commitment to cognition as pure mental operation uncontaminated by feeling, however, means that their categories remain external and formalistic. How, for instance, does one achieve 'comprehension' without, as a prior condition, having a feeling of involvement? How, having achieved comprehension, can one remain unaffected by it? How, in particular, can one manage 'evaluation' – the pinnacle of Bloomian cognition – without commitment to certain values, however rationally derived? But it is on the affective side that the 'domain' theory reveals its spuriousness most clearly. The attempts to define the activity of 'valuing', for instance, uncontaminated by rational thought, verge on the comic. (Holly, 1973, p. 138)

Indeed, such complete regularity is not only undesirable, it is impossibly totalitarian.

However, a purpose of regularity in a course of study is to provide a way of learning which is easier to follow than an unorganized, irregular way. This presumes that *what* is to be learnt is known, and that what is required is the most efficacious way of reaching it for a learner. Bloom's taxonomy is an attempt to articulate with logical precision the kinds or classes into which 'what is to be learnt' can be put; and these in Bloomian terms, can all be subsumed 'hierarchically' in broad 'domains', cognitive, affective and psycho-motor. This is useful so far as it indicates that the word 'curriculum' is to do with the regulation of human experience as a way of *communicating* experience efficaciously. However, Bloom's work is a serious obstacle to the use of the word 'curriculum' in so far as it both externalizes and divides human experience in terms of a by no means indisputable theory of knowledge.

> Is there any knowledge in the world which is so certain that no reasonable man can doubt it? This question, which at first sight might not seem difficult, is really one of the most difficult that can be asked. When we have realised the obstacles in the way of a straightforward and confident answer, we shall be launched on the study of philosophy – (Russell, 1912, opening lines of the work)

Russell was by no means the first, or the last, philosopher to pose this question. Neither he nor others have provided a satisfactory answer. In this perspective the conceptual superstructure of Bloom *et al* lacks a certain foundation. Of course, this was recognized by Bloom, and it was not his purpose to found a theory of knowledge, but rather to bring some sort of order and coherence to the universe of educational discourse about objectives. (The taxonomy is, perhaps, best thought of as a sort of conceptual machine for interpreting an educationalist 'Babel'). In this respect it is crucial to recognize that whether the word 'curriculum' is used in a broad or narrow sense (Goodlad, 1979), it always involves 'regularity', and regularity necessarily implies a directive purpose, aim or objective. The word 'curriculum', therefore, necessarily implies organization, but it does not necessarily imply any particular theory of knowledge, nor any particular learning hierarchy, pedagogy or method.

Now the terms 'purpose', 'aim', objectives' are themselves problematic (fully discussed in Davies, 1976, for example). The important point here is that there is no curriculum which does not have a purpose of some kind, explicit, implicit or accidental. Implicit purpose is a recognized but unexpressed, or partially expressed purpose; whereas, an accidental purpose is neither expressed nor recognized. This latter category of purpose may seem farfetched, but it takes little imagination to sense the likelihood that curriculum outcomes inevitably include more (or perhaps less) than was bargained for by design. This is to include in the notion of purpose, aim or objective, the effect of a regularity which is not part of conscious curriculum design, but is nevertheless operating on the experience of the learner/participant. It is to say that a curriculum can have not only an effective hidden (covert) purpose (or undeclared purpose), but also an 'unconscious' purpose, which is accidentally effective. The taxonomy seems to assume the exclusion of the accidental as if pure models of curriculum were possible in the social world. Such models cannot, and perhaps should not anyway, be realized. Curricula subsist as organizations affecting their members through the mediation of the organization's behaviour on their own individual behaviours. Such an explicit curricular purpose may be declared by an organization's managers (teachers) and a resulting method of acting on the experience of some organization members (learners) be worked out and operated. However, actual organizational behaviour and its effects on individual members may little resemble managers' intentions, hopes or expectations. In other words, managers' purposes may not result in congruent organizational behaviour. Holly's (1973) point is that Bloom's taxonomy is absurdly overambitious. My point is that curricular purpose is managerial organization input, and, as such, an intended influence on or determinant of organization behaviour, and that it is the behaviour of the organization which significantly affects the behaviour of its members. Bloom's taxonomy and the hierarchy can easily result in a totalitarian managerial input into the learning organization. As such it may result in individual behaviours which reflect less the learning objectives and more the totalitarian behaviour of the learning organization. Such totalitarian behaviour is a major unconscious regularity, and can be regarded as an accidental purpose of the learning organization in a 'free society'.

In the perspective of curriculum as organization the notion of purpose can be reduced to the question *'why'*. This is to say that, in part, the word 'curriculum' is involved with the question: Why is a learner's general experience being regularized in the particulars of a course of study? In the English education system it is possible, in the same breath, to speak of subject curricula and *the* curriculum, while at the same time referring to syllabuses. Indeed, several major curricula recognizably subsist in the system. Recognition is possible by distinguishing between the purposes of the regularized educational experiences of pupils. Through this a useful way of using the word 'curriculum' can be determined which accounts for the problematic internal distinctions of subjects/disciplines, as they are organized in the experience of pupils in schools. Drawing such a distinction crucially involves the notion of holism. This is to say, after Goodlad's latter distinction (above), that, irrespective of teachers' subject distinctions, if there is either or both a *general* purpose to the organization of subjects, and temporal contiguity between them in the experience of pupils, then a range of subjects is compoundly experienced by pupils, whether deliberately integrated or not, and that this experience occurs in a curriculum organization.

This latter point does not reject the valuable distinction of Bernstein (1971), between collection and integrated code curricula, which is a sociological one put in organizational terms. It is, however, to argue that, irrespective of a pedagogical strategy of deliberate integration, contiguity between pupils' experiences when doing subject courses is sufficient for them to experience a whole effect (whether this makes much sense to them in terms of a 'logical' whole is *not* the point). Holism in this sense means simply the general experience of a pupil in school in one time-horizon. A time-horizon is more likely to be a week than a term; some speculation about experiential time-horizons might suggest that their duration is age related, shorter horizons being associated more with younger pupils than older.

With this in mind, a fundamental point about a curriculum called *the* secondary school curriculum is its general purpose:

> Close to the heart of any formulation of the aims of education must lie concern to develop the potential of all pupils to enjoy a full personal life and to take an informed and responsible part in the adult world, including their part in the economic life of the country. Curricular provision, therefore, ought not to be such as to shut off any pupils from important areas of knowledge and experience, or to suggest quite different views of their future role in society. The opportunities to learn provided by the school and the nature of the teaching must take account both of individual differences and of essential common needs. Most schools recognise this in principle, and earlier parts of the report describe the complex, often ingeniously contrived organisations through which they seek to provide appropriate curricular programmes ... (HMI, 1979, p. 265)

In this the HMI has retained that somewhat ambiguous, or perhaps ambivalent liberalism often associated with Matthew Arnold. However, avoiding Arnold's general confusion, the HMI retain the important reservation that pupils should not be shut off from important areas of knowledge and experience, but that there should be *included* in these areas their part in the economic life of the country, rather than a training to fit a predetermined role in that life. The HMI refers, too, to ingeniously contrived organizations to provide appropriate curricular programmes.

There is, at present, a general purpose to the secondary school curriculum, which the HMI have found in the practices of the schools in their survey. Essentially, it is to provide pupils with a sensible opportunity to sample a range of specific subject 'syllabuses'. The *curriculum* in this part of the 'regular course of study', therefore, refers not to the individual syllabuses, but to the whole 'menu' experienced by the pupils. This is *the* curriculum for an age range of pupils in secondary schools; it is, therefore, *a* curriculum in the English educational system. As a curriculum it is characterized by 'collection code' organizations regulating, to a significant extent, the learning experience of children entering secondary education to 16 years, although often with 'a marked break at fourteen' (HMI, 1979, p. 265). The present 14–18 initiative, associated directly with the Prime Minister (Mrs Thatcher), to bifurcate the education system using this 'break', would radically change the concept of a comprehensive, liberal, common curriculum available to all pupils.

> We are seeking the establishment ... of full-time integrated courses of technical and vocational education, starting at age fourteen, continuing through the four years to age eighteen, leading to recognised technical qualifications.... This will complement existing opportunities in full-time education and parallel the provision under the Youth Training Scheme next September for those leaving full-time education at sixteen. (Norman Tebbit, Secretary of State for Employment, December 1982, reported in Employment News, No. 103)

The 'marked break' at 14 is already, of course, the point at which the 'liberal curriculum' of the HMI disengages itself in practice from the 'lower half', remaining attached to the inchoate sixth form of two years hence. The 'lower half' usually pick up what was referred to earlier as the 'other' secondary school curriculum, or those 'appropriate curricular programmes' referred to by HMI.

However, the subject pattern of the 'liberal curriculum' is firmly established early on in a structure reinforced by:

> ... the single subject basis of public examinations at sixteen plus. An a la carte examinations system sits more comfortably on an *a la carte* curriculum than would, say, one which required a candidate to enter for a minimum number of subjects or to select them according to certain broad principles in order to qualify for a certificate. The fact that a very much larger proportion of pupils representing a wide range of ability now

enter for at least one or two subjects in public examinations at sixteen, also tends to support a curriculum arrived at by the aggregation of discrete units. (HMI, *op. cit.*, p. 266)

The issue here is that the object of the liberal curriculum to provide a *general* education suffers in practice not only from bifurcation at 14 into a 'two halves' provision, but that the top half provision has an early tendency toward A-level 'disciplinary' specializations which are premature, and effectively, in another way, bifurcate the liberal curriculum into Science and Arts. Indeed, the only clear and serious example of a deliberate attempt to form an integrated curriculum in this respect is that of the international baccalaureate whose '... objective is to provide a general education preparatory to further studies and not a premature and generally illusory specialisation' (Renaud, 1974, p. 34).

This argument against the disintegrative effect of early specialization is echoed by,

> Let us take the commonest pattern of study (the 8–8–3–3–curriculum): the pattern which most fourteen year olds are at present in for if they are eventually going to stay on for a full sixth form course ....

> It is hard to justify such a bizzare shape on theoretical grounds. No one in his senses, given a fourteen-eighteen curriculum to design from scratch, would produce anything quite as odd as this.... (Schools Council, 1972, p. 74, my parenthesis)

There is also another form of 8–8–3–3 (identified *ibid.* as even odder) and the somewhat fallacious Schools Council solution (also *ibid.*) of an 8–8–5–3– curriculum – this inducing a 17+ (intermediate I-level) examination.

The rights and wrongs of all this can be supposed at length, there are plenty of pins and angels to go round. What matters to the discussion at this stage, is that the secondary schools in the HMI survey seriously attempted to deliver a liberal common curriculum. That such delivery is fraught with the problems of delivering certificates to pupils and parents alike, and coping with 'dim' pupils, who can't or won't fit in with the scheme of things, is utterly commonplace to teachers. These practicalities disorganize the ideal, and result in the practice of the 'other curriculum' for the bottom half. This major erosion of the liberal idea at 14+ leads to effective collapse at 16+. Pupils, in spite of such infernal practices, still go to school, sit in the classrooms, walk the corridors, picking up this and that, until they leave to make their fortunes, or otherwise in that curious place the world, sometimes referred to as a labour market.

The essential point being made is that the curricular organization of pupils' time establishes a temporal contiguity between diverse subject matter in short time-horizons. This effectively enables diverse subject material to form part of *the* curriculum organization of which pupils are members. This is to say that a curriculum does not depend on a deliberate overall regularization of its content material (integrated code) so as to be defined as a curriculum. The defining or forming of a curriculum in practice is mainly dependent on the organization of pupils' time. Such organization can be more or less totalitarian depending on the scope of, or the extent to which, time is organized, together with the depth or detail to which the organized time is used to regularize and govern the experience and the individual behaviour of the members of the curriculum organization. The syllabus of a single O-level GCE subject becomes a curriculum, in these terms, for a pupil *if* it is the sole regulated learning experience of that pupil within a time-horizon. In other words, a pupil simply taking, say, O-level divinity in an FE college, and only attending that course, experiences this single subject as a curriculum. If, however, a pupil took three O-levels in the same time-horizon, then their temporal contiguity would cause the curriculum to be comprised of the pedagogy and the syllabus matter of all three subjects. This is not to confine a pupil's experience in a regulated learning situation to that which he is expected or ought to learn (the regulated experience), but to include, as well, the other regulations he experiences as a member of the curriculum organization.

In a real sense a curriculum behaves as an organization, having members, a power/authority structure, a purpose and a regularity of behaviours associated with purpose. Certainly, such an organization may subsist in the wider organization, or rather institutional framework of a school or college, although not necessarily. The pre-16 secondary school curriculum behaves in this way. Its members, teachers and pupils subsist in a basic timetable construct which regulates the learning experience of the pupils. Teachers, of course, often belong to several of these organizations at once in any particular time-horizon, whereas pupils always belong only to one.

Post-16 pupils who remain in secondary schools have several curricula open to them. In the simplest terms a post-16 sixth form curriculum is an organization in which its members experience three A-level GCE subjects (syllabuses), together with sports, social and 'other' studies. In this respect a sixth former's curriculum is *the* curriculum for that particular pupil. Consequently, several kinds of curriculum can be identified in most sixth forms. Whereas in the lower school there are broadly only two kinds of curriculum: organizations for O-level GCE, and the organizations for other, or few, or no, examination pupils; the 'other curriculum'. However, this can be further differentiated by tracing curriculum organizations in terms of such factors as shared contents/levels, shared memberships (the degree to which teachers are shared and pupils are in contact with each other – this could be treated in the simple term of sharing space). Obviously, the more differentiated (individualized) a curriculum organization is, the less its members obtain/perceive organizational identity. The powerful sense of belonging associated with the private boarding school compared to the loose/alienative relationship of pupils to day comprehensives could be isolated in such terms.

As there is usually an array of 'options' in lower school it is possible to argue that there are as many curricula as there are variations to individual pupils' timetables. Nevertheless, the broad distinction between organizations for upper half 'bright' pupils and organizations for lower half 'less bright' pupils is a sufficient and proper distinction to identify two species or kinds of curriculum organizations. In the final analysis, however, *the* curriculum is the regulated learning experience of each pupil as a whole in a fairly short time-horizon. In this perspective, each pupil experiences only *one* curriculum, his own, in any particular time-horizon; and enters and leaves perhaps several organizations during his educational 'life'.

Using this simple holistic approach, based on the regulated learning experience of the pupil, it is a clear, if obvious, point that curricula in the English educational system narrow in scope while increasing in depth as pupils advance in pyramid fashion to an ultimate or leaving point. Although it could be said that the elementary base is one shared by all, this would be to overestimate the degree to which there is an actual national common curriculum at elementary level. What is clear is that there are considerable similarities between the regulated learning experiences of pupils in the curricular organizations delivering *the* elementary curriculum. Nevertheless, it remains the case that each pupil experiences his particular regulated learning experience, and that at elementary level this is an organization of learning in which he subsists, and which is of similar behaviour to many others involved in the common general purpose. Consequently, as each pupil progresses from one 'organization' to the next, his 'pyramid' is to a significant and increasing extent organizationally unique (this is to leave aside that uniqueness dependent on individual difference).

Ultimately, a pupil may enter an organization regularizing his learning experience so that he may become fully engaged with one subject discipline. In this the subject discipline alone provides the regularity to the organization of learning experience, in its own purpose and in the particular time-horizon of the pupil (student). Consequently, the single subject discipline is *the* curriculum. Alternatively, a pupil may enter an organization of learning experience whose purpose is to form vocational expertise; and this is *the* curriculum. Therefore, the 'pyramid' has potentially a multitude of apexes each of which could be described as a 'distinct curriculum'.

It is in this sense that the word 'curriculum' is used herein. At the one point the word refers to learning experience involving several 'subjects' temporally contiguous in the time-horizons of pupils, at another to a single subject, or to a vocational 'course', when these are matters in a single organization of pupils' time-horizons and regularizing their learning experience. The term 'new curriculum' is used throughout as a way of referring to such organization of learning experiences. The term is used putatively during the exploratory, investigative chapters, but nevertheless refers to what might best be described as a new, if inchoate, apex among those already existing to the range of pyramids in the English education system. This is to argue that a regular course of study is rightly referred to as a curriculum and not a syllabus in this respect. The simile of a pyramid should not, of course, be taken as a conceptual model, but rather as providing a perspective sufficiently generalized to avoid being susceptible to simple contraversions, while remaining a reasonably consistent instrument of broad explication. Hence, consideration of apexes does not prevent curricula, so described, leading to others. However, the further an individual gets toward a particular apex, especially if it is vocational in character, the more difficult it becomes to 'change course'.

In formulating a framework for thinking about curriculum design, the Further Education Curriculum Review and Development Unit (FEU) came up with their definition of curriculum:

> The organising principles underlying this review of curriculum design styles are based on the assumption that the real curriculum is what is learned by students. All other statements, syllabuses, documents, committees, visitations, approvals and examinations are processes designed to guide or record that

learning. A series of interactive social processes lies between the central curriculum bodies and the students. These processes influence, guide and possibly control what the student learns. (FEU, March 1981, para. 5, p. 2)

The FEU is, of course, stuck with the large task of trying to describe Further Education curricula. In its work on curriculum control in Further Education (March 1981) the FEU began, as above, by stating that what is learned by a student is a curriculum, and how he comes about learning what he learns is importantly a result of interactive social processes between central curriculum bodies and students. An aspect of these processes is described, and the institutional influences on *aims*, *learning situations* and *assessment* procedures typified. The FEU uses its typology as a way of describing (curricular) phenomena, which can also be, and is, confused with analyzing them.

The approach could almost lead to tidiness and, indeed, a short book about a 'new curriculum' which has centrally controlled aims, locally set 'exams' to national 'standards', and talk of reverse Mode 2, etc. This is not to suggest that descriptive categorization of FE curricula will not prove to be a valuable map for FE managers, that is, a useful management tool. However, it is to say that the FEU approach is not the approach of this book. Here a curriculum is treated as an organization in which the learner subsists, voluntarily or involuntarily, as a member among others in a power/authority structure, where experience is regularized for a purpose explicit, implicit or accidental. Unfashionable as it may be, *what* the learner is intended to learn is not treated herein as the curriculum (and the reification argument is ignored). There is acceptance that the real curriculum is insufficiently described using a form of remote categorization, that such description is marginal in important respects. However, there is adequate recognition, in the perspective taken here of curriculum as organization, of the influential nature of such structural features as *aims*, *learning situations* (methods) and *assessment*. This to say that the behaviour of organizations is certainly importantly related to structure, and that it is a significant determinant of the behaviour of individual organization members, and that included in such individual behaviour is, among other things, what is learned.

It has already been argued that the *why*, or purpose, of a regular course of study is an important determinant of a curriculum. In terms of describing a curriculum the *why* forms an aspect of a non-seriatim or iterative, group of questions: *who*; *why*; *what*; *how*. In treating a curriculum as an organization these questions remain pertinent; indeed the regularities in behaviour of an organization are to do with its goals, both formal, informal and unofficial. A curriculum cannot, therefore, be dissociated from its goals, teachers' goals and pupils', the goals of collective interests, managers, politicians and indeed the organization's own, as it were, homeostatic 'goals'. Involved inextricably with these is the nature, the disposition of its members, the *who*, and their goals and abilities and desires to achieve them. Who the members of a 'curriculum' organization are may be determined to varying degrees by the *why*. Equally, and in any order of precedence (these are all chickens and eggs), the *what*, and the *how*, construct aspects of the regular experience of the learner members.

Throughout this book, curriculum is treated very much in terms of a learning syllabus (content) and pedagogy (procedure and rules) fundamentally ensconced in an organization. It is the totality of the organization, its behaviour, and the behaviour of its members, which is the curriculum. These curricula, as organizations operating in the world of education and training, operate in a world of socio-economic and political pressures, constraints and actions. The Gordian knot, as it were, is dissected with the simple instruments *who, why, what, how*. At this time an approach to curriculum *purely* in terms of organization theory remains firmly on the agenda for future research, and indeed for future conceptional unscrambling from major questions of approach. David Silverman's classic (1970) study of the theory of organizations illustrates both the range and differences of approach to the study of organizations which would need resolution before a truly disciplined study of curriculum in these terms could be contemplated. However, the NTI Youth Training Scheme is itself an *apparently* major departure from traditional post-war training and education. Therefore, it is not without merit to take a new direction for its description and analysis.

Nevertheless, exploring the New Training Initiative in order to find out if, among its general machinations, a 'new curriculum' is, or could be, emerging in the English education system, is carried forward herein upon this rather ad hoc conceptual raft, comprised of the planks *who, what, how, why*. Although not objectively addressed, the raft lands from time to time on the odd jungle clad island, wherein the occasional saber-toothed tiger is encountered.

> 'Don't be foolish!' said the wise old man, smiling most kindly smiles. 'We don't teach fish-grabbing to grab fish; we teach it to develop a generalized agility which can never be developed by

mere training. We don't teach horse-clubbing to club horses; we teach it to develop a generalised strength in the learner which he can never get from so prosaic and specialised a thing as antelope-snare-setting. We don't teach ....

You must know there are some eternal verities, and the saber-tooth curriculum is one of them!' (Benjamin, 1939, in Hooper, 1971, p. 15)

The Youth Opportunities Programme (YOP) taught generalized occupational skills, but it is not to be supposed there was anything saber-toothed about that. Benjamin (1939) was, of course, referring to stick-in-the-mud liberal arts, and dying crafts. Or is the coin for turning? Certainly, the curious predilection of the Newsom coin to turn up bottoms every time may be related to some eternal verity.

Another depressing feature found in these papers as in the Newsom report, is the emphasis on vocational education. There is everything to be said for vocational education, if this means that on leaving school everyone is intellectually equipped to understand what any vocation, 'professional' as well as non-professional, involves. But the only vocations which in either the Newsom report or the Schools Council's are to influence the curriculum of the young school leaver are those in manual or service industries. Why only these? No one can rationally pre-judge that any normal child will never be able to hold down a professional career, so there is no good reason to cut him off from this. True, the economy needs non-professional workers; but there is no good reason to shape most children's education with only economic ends in view. (White, 6 March 1969, p. 360 in Hooper, 1971, pp. 279–80)

2　The Emergence of a 'New Curriculum'

> 'The Walrus and the Carpenter
> Were Walking close at hand;
> They wept like anything to see
> Such quantities of sand:
> 'If this were only cleared away,'
> They said, 'it would be grand!'
> 'If seven maids with seven mops
> Swept it for half a year,
> Do you suppose,' the Walrus said,
> 'That they could get it clear?'
> 'I doubt it,' said the Carpenter,'
> And shed a bitter tear.

Lewis Carroll,
Through the Looking Glass,
Chapter 4

For some years now a 'new curriculum' has threatened to emerge from the dark recesses of reports, proposals, minutes and schemes, and from the various practices of teachers upon the young unemployed. It has threatened to educate and/or to train that great mass of minimum age leavers which has recently encumbered the statistics of the Department of the Employment. Through this gloom the Manpower Services Commission (MSC) has brightly coupled its vast wealth and manpower to indigent industry and importunate further education, bringing forth several generations of training and/or work experience schemes for both jobless youth and those in jobs without training. Indeed, in 1976 the MSC suggested to itself that it might set (itself) the objective of ensuring, 'all young people of sixteen-eighteen years of age who have no job or who are not engaged in further or higher education should have the opportunity of training, of participating in a job creation programme, or of work experience' (MSC, 1976).

In May 1977 it published its feasibility report, *Young People and Work*. Informing this report were important, if now recognized as optimistic, predictions about future youth unemployment and the broad trend of future demand for labour by basic occupational segmentation. The predictions showed a clear upward trend in youth unemployment to 1981 (*ibid*, Table IV, V, VI). In the event the upward trend was steeper, and the long-term unemployment more severe. The downward trend in demand for labour, especially in primary manufacturing and processing of materials (*ibid*, Table VIII) was also more severe than predicted. Nevertheless, the MSC did comprehend the significance of the then incipient collapse of demand for unskilled and unqualified school leavers. In the feasibility report were the germs of YOP, WEEP, UVP, and even the grain of the New Training Initiative (NTI) (MSC, Dec. 1981).

However, the initial position of the MSC in 1977 was based on five major conclusions:

(i) the levels of unemployment for young people with which any new programmes will have to deal over the next years are unlikely to be significantly lower than current levels, although the trend will be downward if unemployment falls generally after 1978;

(ii) whatever the trend from year to year the annual cycle of youth unemployment caused by the influx of school leavers in the Spring and Summer and their gradual absorption into employment in the Autum means that there are sharp fluctuations in unemployment of young people during the course of each year;

(iii) there are likely to be increasing numbers of seventeen and eighteen year olds entering the labour market;

(iv) there are major variations in the scale and nature of employment problems between different parts of the country;

(v) the expected continued fall in demand for certain traditional craft skills will lead to a reduction in the number of long-term trainees in those skills, offset to some extent by an increased demand for technicians and some semi-skilled occupations (but the position will vary considerably between industries). If young people with good qualifications and of high ability, who would formerly have entered skilled jobs, begin to go into less skilled employment, then those with poorer qualifications will encounter more pressure in the job market. (MSC, 1977, p. 23, para. 1.22)

Although these conclusions were correct in the immediate term, they can now be seen, with hindsight, to have been established in a completely different economic perspective than was to become the reality in the 1980s. Nevertheless, important characteristics of the future labour market were discerned. Not least of these was the perception, intimated in (v), that the nature of demand would be increasingly marked by a trend toward the new worker, the all-round occupational technician. With this characteristic was the added and increasing problem of demand-deficiency for the young unskilled in competition with each other on an increasingly tough basis, with low ability/attainment youngsters being significantly displaced from the labour market altogether by those who attained school and college qualifications.

Uncertainty, too, in the estimation of demand for traditional trades in industries facing stepped type change; Food, Drink and Tobacco, for example, was seen as a potentially serious problem. Indeed, in this the MSC tried earnestly for significant sector by sector analysis with its document *Training for (Vital) Skills* (1978? undated). Here, the MSC did identify, perhaps more accurately than even now has been generally recognized, an expected shift in workforce structure. It concluded that the expected pace of change could be calibrated as 'SLOW', 'GRADUAL', 'RAPID', 'STEPWISE', against expected significance of technological change, as 'MAJOR', 'CONSIDERABLE', 'AVERAGE', 'LITTLE', 'NONE' (MSC, 1978? undated, Table 2, Annex 4, p. 36). It predicted, for example, that the British Steel Corporation could expect a rapid to stepwise pace of change with major to considerably significant technological change. This is to say that the *structure* of employment demand would change dramatically, whether general economic demand changed or not. This distinction is one of some significance to the present and future role of the MSC in the formulation of a national training policy, and its implementation. The nature of the labour market, and unemployment in it, and the concepts involved, are discussed below.

Although the MSC's predicted demand quantities for kinds of manpower proved wrong in the event, because of the severe and then unaccounted for downturn in general economic demand, much of its analysis of the future shifting of demand *structure* is still of significance. Indeed, as a backdrop to the book it is worth quoting at some length from Table 3, Annex 4, p. 37 of MSC (1978? undated).

> But because for the more complex machinery introduced, single skill craftsmen will be inadequate: setting and fault finding, for example, will require not only an understanding of mechanical engineering, but also, electrical and electronic engineering: hence a multi-skilled craftsman. (Food, Drink and Tobacco)

> Although the numbers of conventional craftsmen will drop, there will be a demand for highly skilled, broadly based craftsmen/technicians. (Aerospace)

> The indications are that industry's future requirements will not be met simply by training more people in current technical skills using current curricula etc.... The real significance lies in fewer but higher calibre personnel.... (Chemicals)

> Supervisors and plant operators will require to be skilled in fault-finding, as fast, integrated processes become more common and the consequences of breakdowns are intensified. They will need a basic understanding of the relevant process to do this, as well as the ability for independent and creative thinking. (Paper, Print, Publishing and Packaging) (MSC, 1978?, p. 37)

Irrespective, then, of general economic demand, the *nature* of demand for labour was predicted to change substantially in the 1980s. In this respect the MSC's concentration on purely the labour market and the nature of the 'new' working man is salutary. Young people leaving school or college would in any case find themselves facing employers who needed fewer employees, but those they would need would have to meet both wider and, at the same time, deeper and more complex requirements. Skilled workers would need a broader understanding of the overall technology or process rather than a manual dexterity. They would need to know *how* a machine works, and be capable of diagnostic and problem-solving skills. The requirement here is not simply an updating retraining process, but a fundamental shift to higher calibre personnel capable of becoming multi-skilled tradesmen. Semi-and unskilled workers will be affected in two ways. There will be a tendency for their work to be further deskilled as production lines become increasingly automated, and responsibility for the purely manual input to products is pushed back as far as possible to the producing country or company. However, there will be some opportunity for a moderate increase in skills to reach a level below craft skills in occupations such as monitoring and testing in automated processes. In general, however, the traditional craft skills section of the workforce will face the most significant decline in demand. In this context, too, apprentice training was generally held to be of excessive duration, too narrowly based and inflexible.

The MSC's response on the training front was massively geared to adult (prime-age males 24 to 55 years) retraining and development. Skills centres, colleges, polytechnics and even universities were used to deliver the Training Opportunities Scheme (TOPS). However, youth was not neglected. As already pointed out, MSC special programmes were established to 'cope' with the youth unemployment problem. Herein, the MSC founded its key concept for training unemployed young people upon four basic types of opportunity. These included a special measure, which continues to date, to provide help for seriously disadvantaged young people and those who found it difficult to hold down jobs. This remains the waged Community Industry Programme. The other three approaches were formed under a broad concept for improving the employability of young people. These were short work preparation courses, work experience (courses), and a system of incentive training grants. The last provision was geared to fund training which could be identified specifically to meet anticipated requirements for manpower at higher skill levels. In essence, therefore, two broad types of modes of opportunity formed the real basis for MSC funded/provided training for the young unemployed: work preparation and work experience. It is within the processes of work preparation and work experience courses that the fundamentals of a pre-vocational curriculum were congregated, developed and experienced by trainers and trainees. In addition, vocational education and training was later provided through the Unified Vocational Preparation Scheme for young people in jobs which in themselves provided neither.

The courses originally formulated for the young unemployed were eventually partially integrated under the Youth Opportunities Programme (YOP) as a constructive alternative to unemployment. There were broadly seven courses in five modes. In the preparation mode:

1 assessment and employment induction courses of two weeks' duration;

2 short industrial courses of about thirteen weeks' duration;
3 remedial and preparatory courses of indeterminate duration to meet individual needs;

and, in the work experience mode;

4 about six months on employers' premises;
5 project-based, of up to twelve months' duration;
6 training workshops, of up to twelve months' duration;
7 community service projects, of up to twelve months' duration.

All these course titles are now recognizable components of various extensions and developments coming later in MSC inspired schemes for young people. They were components, too, of an inchoate pre-vocational preparation curriculum.

Such training through the MSC was clearly intended to prepare the young unemployed for work as a way of solving the youth unemployment 'problem'. This problem, of course, was, and is, part and parcel of the whole unemployment problem, and solutions to it involve aspects of solutions to the whole unemployment problem. The youth unemployment problem was largely treated, and presumably seen, in terms of the analysis that, whatever the level of general demand for labour, the nature of demand was shifting structurally. Consequently, whether the general level of unemployment could be reduced by training or not, training was in any case needed to ensure that demand for the 'new' skills could be met. Involved with this was the simple effect of reducing the general level of unemployment by defining (not counting) those unemployed in training schemes as employed. However, the question of how to define and measure unemployment involves more significant processes than simple manipulation, and has been the subject of serious research and analysis as well as the cosmetics of political 'treatments'. In his seminal 1975 article, 'How to Measure Unemployment', John Hughes distinguished between several key forms of unemployment. Because unemployment has been, and now is, crucially, the central stimulus for MSC action in the post-16 curriculum field, it is important to analyze its character. Such analysis is important in two respects. First, in relation to questions about the future demand for such MSC initiatives (responses); and, second, in relation to the nature of the aims or purposes for such training; in other words, the *WHY*.

Hughes' general analysis is of arguments that unemployment

figures are deceptive, in the sense that they give an inflated impression of the amount of actual unemployment. This argument was most forcefully put by Sir Keith Joseph in September 1974 when he expressed the view that for much of the time we had negative real unemployment, a shortage of labour, although the statistics gave the impression otherwise. This point was related to his thesis that inflation was a 'self-inflicted wound' caused by governments expanding aggregate demand through deficit financing in order to reduce the number of registered unemployed. Hughes concluded that if this diagnosis is correct then,

> ... given that inflation is to be tackled seriously, the implication is that the economy ought to be operated at a higher – perhaps much higher – level of registered unemployment than has been customary over the last thirty years or so. (Hughes, 1975, p. 317)

Essentially, the moral basis for such an economic strategy importantly depends on the idea that the figures for unemployment are actually deceptive, and do not indicate a reality of mass socio-economic deprivation *caused* by a *real* general situation of unemployment. This is to assume that the ethics of operating the economy with *deliberate* intent to cause large numbers of people to suffer such deprivation to be, at the least, morally incompetent, if not simply wrong. Consequently, the question of how to measure unemployment, and the effective answer to it, is central to a determination of both the economic reality and the morality of a deliberate economic strategy involving, as a necessary concomitant, high levels of unemployment. And, an important relation to this, is the matter of the aims of MSC youth programmes, and their conglomerate 'curricula' in the context of levels of aggregate and segmented demand for labour dependent on the whole operation of the economy.

At the heart of Hughes' (1975) analysis are the distinctions between frictional, structural, seasonal and demand-deficient unemployment. Demand-deficient unemployment comes about because of an inadequacy in aggregate demand, and has been traditionally thought of (since Keynes) as susceptible to expansionary demand policies. Frictional unemployment arises when workers move from one job to another, and is thought of as short-term unemployment, and can only exist alongside an unsatisfied demand for labour. Structural unemployment,

> ... arises from a more fundamental mis-match in the labour market. Individual skills become obsolete, or less widely demanded, as a result of structural change – that is change resulting from changes in consumer tastes, production techniques or the location of industry. The individuals possessing these skills will remain unemployed unless their skills can be adapted to new requirements. (Hughes, 1975, p. 318)

Seasonal unemployment results from seasonal changes in economic activity. It may be categorized as frictional if aggregate demand is adequate, if not, then it forms part of demand-deficient unemployment.

Underlying all these distinctions is the broader distinction between voluntary and involuntary unemployment of Keynesian vintage. Keynes defined voluntary unemployment as (in simple terms) unemployment caused by the unwillingness of a worker to accept employment at lower real wages. Involuntary unemployment exists where there is an excess of supply of labour at a given money wage, and its elimination depends both on an expansion of aggregate demand and a reduction in the real-supply price of labour. Hughes believes that Keynes would have included structural unemployment in the category of involuntary unemployment. For Keynes, full employment is the absence of involuntary unemployment, but not frictional (which includes seasonal) and those parts of other forms of unemployment which are voluntary. Full employment is 'a situation in which aggregate employment is inelastic in response to an increase in effective demand for its output' (Keynes, 1936, p. 26).

The key distinction is between structural and demand-deficient unemployment. The creation of a general demand for goods (home produced) in the economy may be formed by deficit financing (artificially?), or by a (natural?) free market demand caused by price competitiveness in the world economy. What is important is that whichever way (and they are not mutually exclusive) demand is manifested, the unemployment that remains is either structural (and involuntary) or voluntary. Structural unemployment, of course, can only exist if there is an unsatisfied demand for labour, and labour exists, but of the wrong skills or in the wrong place, or both. Hughes supports the view that this form of unemployment is, in theory at least, a severe form of frictional unemployment. He points out,

> Whereas both frictional and structural unemployment can increase independent of the level of aggregate demand, both can

be reduced without any expansion in (general economic) demand, provided, of course that the appropriate policy measures are adopted. (Hughes, 1975, p. 318)

Herein lies the nub that, whatever else is done about unemployment in terms of general economic strategy, specific public policy measures may provide practical benefits in dealing with severe frictional (structural) unemployment which is, by definition, involuntary. Hughes notes, 'Those in favour of changing the basis of measuring unemployment are motivated by a desire to see government less willing to expand aggregate monetary demand in order to combat unemployment' and 'If less can be expected of demand-management policies then more will be expected of manpower policy' (Hughes, 1975, p. 331).

Such manpower policy, Hughes recognizes, can only be effectively managed in the long and medium term if sufficient information is available upon which predictive extrapolations of considerable precision can be made about the structure of future skills demands, and that such forecasts about the labour market should be on both a national and a local basis. Santosh Mukherjee (1974) in an equally, if even more premonitory, seminal analysis of unemployment and manpower policies, made this most pertinent of points (to both Hughes' analysis and the subsequent training intervention strategy of the MSC):

> The first thing to be said is that the idea of objective forecasts illuminating the decision-making process must simply be forgotten for the time being. Once that is accepted the strategic issue is determined. Since likely future shortages cannot be identified with any assurance, the thing to do is to keep a vigilant watch on current behaviour of skill markets and to be ready to throw in a big effort to get a throughput of skilled people as soon as it is evident that a shortage is beginning to become particularly uncomfortable. This involves a primitive kind of forecasting and it is forecasting on a very short time horizon. (Mukherjee, 1974, p. 36)

It was against this sort of background that the MSC was formed and began to formulate its national manpower strategy. At this point it is sufficient to note that recognition of the fallibility of manpower forecasting necessarily results in a strategy which fundamentally involves rapid response to short-term forecasts, through a capacity to establish appropriate training on a very fast delivery.

Quite clearly, the English education system is not at all geared to rapid change on its own initiative, and there was/is a need for the agency of the MSC in this respect. Also, the political imperatives for 'adjustment' of the measurement of unemployment, and other such cosmetics, do not alter the underlying value of the distinction between demand-deficient and structural (or severe frictional) unemployment. The term 'frictional' is normally applied to those unemployed who are between leaving one job (voluntarily or involuntarily) and beginning another. This concept extends to structural unemployment on the basis that if adequate manpower policy measures exist to retrain those who are structurally unemployed, then they are only involuntarily unemployed for the period of skill adjustment. If they do not become employed after retraining, and that training was a correct measure, then they are either voluntarily unemployed, or there is an unexpected or unpredicted demand-deficiency (this latter would obviously mean that the policy measure was not, in the event, the correct one).

However, the problem even of determining which skills are presently in demand in any locality, let alone likely to be in the short-term future, is an exceedingly complex one. The complexity derives from the 'Balkanization' of labour markets (Kerr, 1954) and the effective segmentation of the market by occupation and geography (lack of mobility). In other words, the demand for bricklayers may not be satisfied by less than the experienced (unionized) apprenticed tradesmen (Balkanized), a skill-centre man not being deemed good enough; and, even with traditionally high geographic mobility, may not be satisfied by bricklayers living more than thirty miles from site (unless exceptional inducements are offered). The general mobility of labour is low, this is to say, both geographic and skill mobility. The Balkanization theory also argues that the inter-employer mobility of the industrial worker is low. This results from the seniority rules effect which enables industrial workers to accrue non-transferable benefits with one employer, and results in a protective union posture, and a severe reluctance on the part of senior workers to go to another employer and lose their seniority rights. (Employers connive in this in order to prevent ad hoc 'poaching', and local wage spirals, when industrial labour is short).

These intimations should suffice to indicate that manpower policy has to address problems far more complex and intractable than might be apparent at first sight. Such complexity, and indeed uncertainty, makes the formation of specific policy measures somewhat hazardous. This is especially so where decisions are made about what training

should be provided, where, when and for whom. In other words th«
why of a training measure is necessarily formulated from uncertain anc
complex labour market data. The natural tendency is, therefore,
toward measures which react to actual unemployment, in the uncertain
context of forecasted demands for particular skills. The purposes of
training initiatives for unemployed youth are consequently fraught
with questions. Are measures actually aimed at structural aspects of
youth unemployment? Is youth (in any case) structurally or demand-
deficient unemployed? Or is youth, as seems likely at present, demand-
deficient unemployed, but on the basis that a resurgent demand will be
structurally changed. Indeed, the last seems to be the general assumption. In an upturned economy demand for unskilled and semi-skilled
labour will remain deficient, in terms, at least, of the global supply of
this kind of labour. 'Parking' unemployed youth in 'off-the-statistics'
schemes, which do not improve their potential for skilled work, will
not structure provision for the future supply of demands for skilled
labour, and will probably, in fact, oversupply what is presumed to be a
permanently deficient demand for unskilled workers. Conversely, the
fallibility of predictions of precise manpower requirements, in any
respect of the labour market, militates against identifying specific job
skills in advance of virtually the immediate term.

That youth unemployment is probably demand-deficient in the
immediate term, but to be newly structured in the medium term, is the
essential assumption. Consequently, to identify specific job skills
requires a medium-term prediction, which, as already argued, is
fraught with difficulties. Indeed, the record of the MSC, and the many
and various institutions involved with such forecasting, is, with
hindsight, quite startlingly erroneous. For example, the Mukherjee
(1974) projections were regarded, at the time, as almost ridiculously
pessimistic; in the event he proved 'ridiculously' optimistic.

> Thus the 1967 recession brought with it a steep increase in the
> numbers unemployed for given levels of output. The 1973
> events aggravated this situation. As a result, the most optimistic
> hypothesis about future developments is that unemployment
> levels will hover around those experienced over the period
> 1967–69. Looked at from a pessimistic angle, on the other
> hand, 1974 and the two or three years following that might well
> produce levels of unemployment approaching 1.2 million.
> (Mukherjee, 1974, p. 7)

The now generally accepted thesis is that recessionary unemployment 'explosions' or 'shake-outs', although demand-deficient, only tend to fall, in response to an increase in aggregate demand, to higher plateaus than they started from. This is to say that when demand has cyclically caused unemployment to drop, the drops have, since the late 1960s, been less and less, leaving, as it were, 'normal' unemployment at increasingly higher levels. In relation to this, it was recognized as a possibility, even in 1975, that,

> ... the fact that the characteristics of the unemployed in 1973 were so similar to those in 1964 is relevant. It may well be possible that the economy is now less viable than before, in the sense that it can no longer support such full employment without running into balance of payments difficulties or un-acceptable rates of inflation; but there is at present no really hard evidence that the people on the register are any different, or that the statistics have been seriously misleading about the number of men seeking work. (*Department of Employment Gazette*, March 1975, p. 182)

Mukherjee's (1974) analysis supports this view, as does subsequent experience.

In this general context, the up-to-date interpretation of the labour market situation by the MSC adds certain additional concrete facts pertinent to the aims of its youth oriented initiatives, and to the question of the future demand for such initiatives. These are an important addition to its confirmation of the Mukherjee (1974) finding, and prediction, that there is increasingly an inner and outer labour market constructed upon age dimensions, yielding a form of structural unemployment for young and old (in the outer market). Young and old unskilled do not 'compete' successfully against prime-age males, who are in fact clearly preferred by employers.

There are, then, two key additional aspects involved in the present labour market situation. First,

> Unemployment has risen particularly quickly among the craft and other skilled manual occupations; in the twelve months to September 1980 the number unemployed in this group rose by more than eighty per cent (compared with a rise in total unemployment of just over forty per cent), and their share of total unemployment had increased from nine to twelve per cent. Other noticeable effects were the large number of unem-

ployed school leavers in July 1980 in spite of the success of YOP (Youth Opportunities Scheme). (MSC, March 1981, para. 2.6)

and,

... structural change in employment will continue, with further movement towards occupations requiring education, advanced skills or technical training. (*ibid*, para. 2.22)

The prospects are that there will be, at least a medium-term if not permanent, continued demand–deficiency for manual skills in traditional crafts and in the unskilled and semi-skilled labour markets. This demand–deficiency is importantly structural (and therefore involuntary) in character.

The second important aspect is that unemployment is almost certain not to fall in the medium term, it is more likely to increase, and if it does fall, it will not fall by much. There are eight main forecasting bodies for total unemployment. The most accurate, so far as track record is concerned to date, has been the Cambridge Economic Policy Group (CEPG). It forecasted the three million, mid-1982, continuing to rise in linear fashion, to 4.3 million by 1985 (MSC, *Manpower Review 1981*, p. 18). In such circumstances the 'outer labour' market will certainly expand even more than it has in the recent past. Accepting the main point about predictions (of Mukherjee, 1974 above) does not rule out the commonsense impression that if unemployment does not in fact get worse, then it is extremely unlikely that it will get better over the next few years. Indeed, a statistical fall may not be very revealing of the reality. In October 1982 the basis of the unemployment count was changed following the change to voluntary registration at Job Centres. The count in November 1982 and since has been based on those unemployed who have registered at unemployment benefit offices. Under this system the count is lower, although the trend remains similar. The immediate effect was to reduce the count by about a quarter of a million. The nature of unemployment may also become increasingly obscured as people give up, especially those in the outer labour market. Simple assumptions about the behaviour of the unemployed both in a labour market context and in terms of their tractability to national manpower policy instruments may be short-lived.

So far as the prospects and aims of the MSC's special policy measures for young unemployed are concerned, the following points are central.

1 Prospects for continuation and development of special policy measures for young unemployed are high in the medium term.

2 The special training measures are not likely to be temporary, and the proposals for the New Training Initiative are not likely to lead to curricular ephemera, as some past measures have.

3 The MSC's requirement for quick response, in terms of training (and other special measures) interventions in the labour market, will continue to prevail upon the English education system for quick delivery of specified curricula. Equally, the MSC will be less concerned than the education system, particularly FE, with stability through long-term commitments.

4 The emergent curriculum for young unemployed people is likely to persist, and in consequence become even more subject to educational scrutiny, both as a new phenomenon, and as part of the whole range of 16–19 curricula.

5 Although varying from locality to locality, there is likely to be significant structural shift in any upturned demand for young workers. This will be away from the job-specific manual skills inherent in some traditional crafts, and toward high-technology-based work, demanding a broader all round capability to 'manage' technological procedures for operating and/or maintaining automated processes. Such structural shift will certainly apply in manufacturing and to a significant extent in the service sector, as information technology burgeons, for example.

6 Young people will be easily trapped in the 'outer labour' market, unless they can acquire both work knowledge and experience in some degree, to enable them to compete with the preferred prime-age male. Significant failure in this could result in young people forming a permanent caucus in the outer market.

7 There is notorious lack of reliability about manpower requirement predictions in the specifics of both particular job skills and the locality of demand. This is unlikely to improve significantly for more than very short-term prediction. Consequently, there is likely to be a permanent uncertainty about which specific job skills training will lead trainees to definite employment in particular jobs.

Until the YTS proposals, work preparation and work experience courses, congregated under YOP, were the main MSC policy instrument operating in the youth labour market. The emergent 'new curriculum', adumbrated by the latest MSC initiative proposals, is the subject of detailed description and analysis in later chapters. However, it is worth drawing attention now to one significant implication of the foregoing points about the prospects and aims of the MSC's special measures for unemployed youth. This is to do with the features of structural change in demand, together with the expected extended duration of the youth unemployment problem (as part of the whole outer labour market problem).

What seems to be involved is a case of severe frictional unemployment which is significantly demand-deficient, and involuntary on both counts. The strategic remedy involves reducing the income expectations and enhancing the experience and the skills of young people, so they may compete effectively with preferred prime-age males. It also involves training young people to fit the new structure of demand. In addition, there is the need for a new economic context creating adequate aggregate demand. It is clear that none of these aspects of a strategic remedy can be achieved in the short term. Consequently, even when, after a year of training and experience, young people reappear in the labour market, aggregate demand is not likely to have recovered sufficiently in the short term to ensure the year of training, and reduced income expectations, will be enough to make them competitive with prime-age males. It is, therefore, fundamentally doubtful whether one year of training can provide either adequate structural shift in the potential young workforce, or sufficient experience acquisition for them to compete effectively in a demand-deficient market except with each other. An instrument which has the limited aim of removing young people from the market for one year and then returning them is, in this context, highly questionable, unless an upsurge in aggregate demand is expected in the short term, which it is not.

The ineffectiveness of this instrument to achieve the short-term national manpower policy aim of reducing youth unemployment can be, and perhaps should be, related to broader educational issues. A 'new curriculum' providing less for jobs than for individuals is possible in the context of such a short-term instrument of national manpower policy which *cannot* achieve its aim outside a resurgence in aggregate demand. This is to say, that if the measure cannot be efficacious in its short-term manpower aims, it does not follow that it could not contribute to longer-term individual educational development, coupled to a long-term and more complex manpower policy aim. Such an aim need not in itself be *simply* a reason to shape most children's education with only economic ends in view; because such reasoning is involved it need not be *all* that is involved. However, the politics of installing such an aim are complex in the extreme, and explored in more detail in subsequent chapters. This is not to suggest that installation is impossible. Indeed, when such an aim is held by such a significant influence as the Further Education Curriculum Review and Development Unit (FEU), there is *some* marginal prospect of its eventual incorporation in one way or another into what is actually delivered at the chalk-face, presuming, of course, that the further education service will itself be a major provider of chalk, which is now by no means certain.

> But, it is important again to stress that no educational theory or curriculum framework can directly create jobs for young people. It is not suggested that the concept of vocational preparation is a panacea for youth unemployment; it offers ways of improving the provision of education and training, in the hope that it will assist and enrich the transition of young people from school to adult life and thus make them more resilient to uncertainty. (FEU, June 1982, p. vii, para. 4)

Resilience may indeed be the operative word.

The IMS (1981) has already argued the present existence of an outer-outer labour market for young people in London, a point not without relevance to the FEU view of YTS.

> With the probability of youth jobs becoming increasingly uncertain, indeed one major piece of research summarized elsewhere (IMS, 1981a) seriously questions the existence of young people's jobs as a distinct and permanent classification, it is perhaps no longer possible to consider vocationally specific courses as the main way in which the FE System should prepare young people for work. (FEU, Nov. 1982, p. 2, para. 8)

In parallel with MSC inspired training developments in this sphere went a multiplicity of investigations, reports and proposals in another sphere, which can best be described as comprised of the highly assorted spectrum of organized educational interests, particularly those involved with, responsible for, connected with or otherwise associated with 16–19 curricula. Considerable questioning of the education system followed the period of comprehensive reorganization in the late 1960s (DES Circular 10/65). This was a questioning of the secondary school curriculum.

Up to this time the problems had been seen almost exclusively in terms of the structure and organization of secondary schools, but by now it was apparent that such questions had to be considered in conjunction with the content of the curriculum. Even the most 'progressive' comprehensive schools had tended to operate with a watered down version of a grammar school curriculum or an uneasy amalgamation of elementary and grammar curricula. Very few comprehensive schools had thought out their curriculum from first principles (Lawton, 1975, p. 4)

Of course, concern remains for the way 16–19 curricula are organized, especially in relation to the problem of declining rolls and shrinking traditional sixth forms. This concern was often manifested in the vexed and much vested question of tertiary versus sixth form colleges, and has been discussed very fully in Cotterell and Heley (1981), for example. A major government assessment of this problem culminated in the Macfarlane Report (December 1980) which, among other things, concluded that cost effectiveness should be an important organizing principle. Nevertheless, the relevance of traditional curricula and the examination system to the needs of society has in the last ten years become a major agenda item in its own right, and superseded the organizational question in importance.

While this was initially, and is still largely, confined to questioning the whole secondary school curriculum in terms of its socio-political conception and practice, it also extended to serious doubts about the relevance of a subject structured, higher education defined curriculum for the large majority of minimum age leavers (and many 17- and 18-year-old leavers). Wide ranging interests of normally divergent educational and political views were able to agree, perhaps for opposite reasons, that a 'new curriculum' was required. As it happened, much opinion located itself behind changing the examination system as *the* way of 'changing' the secondary school curriculum. The logic of cause and effect seemed inescapable – examinations are the main shapers of the 14–18 curriculum in secondary schools; to change this curriculum therefore requires a change in the examination system, and so on. Curriculum was in many respects not in itself addressed. It is important to recognize that radical opinion wished to change the process of examination as a whole and conservative opinion sought to provide alternative examination. In effect a new curriculum was desired by all sections of opinion, and agreement could be reached, providing the ambiguity between a new curriculum as replacement and a new curriculum as alternative to the then secondary school curriculum was not resolved. Resolution at a political level is presently (1983) occurring on the basis of forming an *alternative* curriculum. Conservative interests tend to see the need in terms of training the 'bottom half' for useful 'followership', to draw a phrase from Eaglesham (1967). On the other side of the coin, in unholy alliance, so to speak, a 'new curriculum' was and is seen as an aspect, or a first step, to wider change; as a way of 'declassing' the university subject dominated path to socio-economic advance. This goes alongside 'a recognition that the curriculum is [sic] a social construction could initiate change in schools with wide ranging social consequences' (Young and Whitty, 1977, p. 9).

Of course, this is a somewhat simplistic assessment of an exceedingly complex range of interactions. Nevertheless, a need was identified for a curriculum 'relevant' to the needs of young people and society. Various attempts were made to modify or change the secondary curriculum and the examination system. A review of the work of the Schools Council alone reveals some of the large-scale attempts and failures to do this. However, in the further education sector considerable change has occurred. In this sector, with its extraordinarily diverse curricula and links with the MSC, there has been considerable actual change in both the management and the content of the system in the last few years. These changes are especially related to the formation of the Technician Education Council (TEC), the Business Education Council (BEC), and to the stimulus and initiative of the MSC's Training Services Division (TSD) in identifying and funding specific training which was often implemented by further education colleges.

Within the general flux of such intensive and extensive curricular activity, the Further Education Curriculum Review and Development Unit (FEU) was established in 1977. The focus of much of its work to date has been on youth training. Arising from this were substantial and influential papers cognate with the larger part of the work actually being carried out for the MSC by further education colleges. The work of the FEU is of great significance, and will be explored in detail later. At this point it is sufficient to recognize that 'relevant' education was being sought across the educational board, and within the system being obstructed by important interests dependent on (and being) the present organizational and administrative paraphernalia of secondary curricula, or dependent on their outcomes.

Certainly, there was broad agreement that in excess of half of all leavers were not adequately catered for by the traditional secondary system, and left insufficiently prepared for a working life. There was not, and is not, broad agreement for radical change in the secondary curriculum. The latest developments, associated with the New Training Initiative and the MSC, are related to a general move by government to establish an express or explicit common national alternative secondary curriculum. The present state of secondary curricula is largely a response of the schools and teachers to the examination system. It reflects, too, the tradition of teacher and local authority autonomy and opposition against the idea of central government control over the curriculum. Such local autonomy was established by the 1902 Act and broadly affirmed through to the 1944 Act.

A general debate on greater involvement for the central authorities in the school curriculum was initiated by Prime Minister James Callaghan in 1976, and found explicit expression in the 1980 DES Green Paper. It was noted in a Royal Institute of Public Administration working party report on education policy in 1980 that:

> It is an interesting reflection on the nature of educational policy debate that just as some Chief Education Officers ... were deploring the centralizing tendency of the new rate support grant arrangements, others were apparently supporting moves for greater central influence on the curriculum, claiming that the present system is one that is 'not far short of 104 local options with any similarity between the provisions in different areas becoming purely coincidental'. (RIPA, 1981, p. 195)

Lawton (1980) provides an interesting and helpful analysis of the development of central government 'intervention' in the school curriculum since the Great Debate (arising from the 1976 Ruskin Speech of the then Prime Minister James Callaghan). Essentially, the July 1977 DES consultative document, *Education in Schools*, set the scene for a centralizing process. To do this the Secretaries of State put the LEAs on the spot by asking them what their schools were in fact doing, what were their curricula.

> The national level the Secretaries of State are responsible in law for the promotion of education of the people of England and Wales. They need to know what is being done by LEA's and, through them, what is happening in the schools. They must draw attention to national needs if they believe the education system is not adequately meeting them. (Lawton, 1980, p. 43)

However, LEAs, while stimulated to open up the 'secret garden' (*ibid*) of their schools' curricula, have fundamentally resisted the centralizing process. This resistance is, perhaps, less a matter of formal local policies than

> ... it is not that simple, as these are two different governments which have both shared responsibilities and separate responsibilities in the same area of endeavour, stemming from the same basic laws. They have different powers, too, which are sometimes wielded in concert and sometimes in opposition to each other... For local government, the operation of the educational system is largely a pragmatic matter of initiation and response, negotiation and settlement within the constraints on action found in particular situations. The central government may then be perceived as one potential constraint among several as local authorities carry out their responsibilities for education. (Jennings, 1977, p. 11)

Nevertheless, central government had, in broad alliance with the Schools Inspectorate (a body of considerable influence – see HMI, 1980, *A View of the Curriculum*) reached a point when it was abundantly clear that central government would give, as it were, a 'lead' to provide a common structure for the curriculum. Fenwick and McBride (1981, pp. 215–25) report the development of this 'lead' and note,

> The new framework, or central direction, is almost finalized in early 1980, but the tone and content of the Conservative ministerial statement echoes the Ruskin speech of 1976. The debate continues, not between parties but between the government in office on the one hand and the profession and the public on the other. (*ibid.*, pp. 224–5).

There is a sense, then, in which it can be argued that the secondary curriculum has been beyond party politics. Certainly, there are major ideological differences between the two main parties, but this manifested itself in terms of arguments about the organization and financing of the state provided sector of education and the public schools system. The arguments were less about what should be taught, than the nature of access to what is taught and the 'quality' and resourcing of the providing institutions. This apparent, and indeed curious, continuity between successive Labour and Conservative governments has been noted somewhat acidly by Marxist educationalists, for example:

Even for the Marxists of the British Communist Party the problem, as with Halsey's 'egalitarian elitism', is one of *access*, not ideology. The problem of class in British education is for them that working-class children are denied what 'our best schools offer'. . . . Thus, the superficially unlikely alignments between conservative educationalists, such as Rhodes Boyson, and the Communist leadership within the National Union of Teachers becomes less surprising. (Young and Whitty, 1977, p. 5)

It has been possible, therefore, for the DES to produce its March 1981 paper, *The School Curriculum*, offering guidance to the LEAs and schools in England and Wales on how the school curriculum can be further improved. Significantly, the Secretaries of State are clear that they will exercise their powers '. . . to inform themselves in due course about the action which, within the resources available to them, local authorities are taking in the light of the guidance in this paper' (DES, March 1981, p. 20, para. 62). The action referred to is for LEAs to ensure that their schools formally express their curricula in writing. It would not be presumptuous to suspect that most schools will find the views of the Secretaries of State of great interest and perhaps relevance in this respect. It seems unlikely that the curricular aims of schools will differ substantially from those of the Secretaries of State. Of course, any substantial differences which did emerge from such an exercise would doubtless prove of immense interest to the Secretaries of State. This is a significant reassertion of the influence of the centre over what is taught in schools. Apart from this 'improvement', there is strong reference to preparation for working life and the desirability of closer links between schools and industry, together with development of the curriculum to include encouragement and advice for pupils in relation to vocational preparation. The paper specifically commends the recommendations made in *Education for 16–19 Year Olds* (DES, Jan. 1981), which would include knowledge of, and skills in deciding about, the world of work in the curriculum.

However, while encouraging innovation in respect of vocational preparation, implicit in the document is an affirmation of traditional subject structured HE defined curricula and examination. Improvements in the teaching of subjects are sought by the Secretaries of State, together with modernization of their contents, particularly in relation to the need for pupils to acquire essential skills in literacy, numeracy, science and technology. There is also concern that 'every pupil up to sixteen should sustain a broad curriculum', and that between eleven and sixteen pupils are provided with curricula of broadly common character, designed to ensure a balanced education which prevents subsequent choices being needlessly restricted. Consequently, a new secondary school curriculum is by no means indicated, albeit that a new 'subject' is intimated, namely vocational preparation. This 'subject' is in fact to be largely aimed at a target group of those pupils who cannot, or do not look likely to, succeed in the traditional structure. This is made explicit in *17+: A New Qualification* (DES, May 1982).

That vocational preparation can at this stage be treated as a 'subject' at all is an indication of the ambiguity surrounding its possible role in secondary schools. Of course, there is considerable scope for such a 'subject' to operate as a kind of mediating process in the present subject structured curriculum. It could take up position as a timetable subject (say two hours per week), or it could take up a whole timetable for the 'bottom half' and form an (the) alternative curriculum, replacing the present 'other' curriculum. In this latter sense the 'subject' vocational preparation would provide an alternative to the 'other' curriculum, and could therefore be regarded not as a subject, but as a (new) curriculum. Such a curriculum could presumably form a part basis for advancing the New Technical and Vocational Education Initiative (NTVEI). What is implicit in *The School Curriculum* (DES, March 1981) is explicit in *17+ A New Qualification* (DES, May 1982), in which the 'target group' for the Certificate in Pre-Vocational Education (CPVE) is identified.

> It excludes young people who have the potential to take two or more A level examinations; and those who have a clear vocational objective which would best be pursued by immediately following a vocational course in further education. The Secretaries of State consider that the target group should be further limited by excluding those who are properly advised to devote their main effort to obtaining or improving GCE O-level or CSE qualifications with a view to gaining access to particular courses or to certain categories of employment. (DES, May 1982, para. 3)

Consequently, the need for 'relevance' in the school curriculum (allied, as always, with the notion of 'standards') could be satisfied by a special subject for the 'less bright' leading to a pre-vocational leaving certificate, while the 'bright' could continue in the traditional framework somewhat 'improved' by concern for relevance to industry and 'wealth creation'.

> The real sadness of the paper's recommendations is, as has already been said, that they divide when they ought to unite and close doors when they ought to open them. There are to be A-level/I-level academic goats (the few) bound for higher education and leadership and the pre-vocational sheep (the many) who will hew wood and draw water preferably well satisfied with their lot. The headline to an article on seventeen-plus in the *Daily Telegraph* dated 3rd December 1981 says it all: 'seventeen-plus pupils to have examinations on cars and catering'. (FEU, Sept. 1982, Macintosh, H., p. 53, para. 5.7)

The somewhat insidious distinction between school or secondary provided pre-vocational preparation, and that provided by further education, depends subtly on whether it is a special MSC (Department of Employment) programme, or a DES/LEA 'official' course. This distinction is explored more fully in subsequent chapters. However, it is worth noting at this point a key feature of the situation. The official providers of education, the DES/LEA's, through secondary schools and FE colleges, have been confronted with a powerful competitor, in the form of the MSC's Training and Special Programmes Division, wheeling and dealing very effectively in a field ostensibly to do with training (not education), and funded by:

> ... central government, especially under the Labour Governments of 1974–9, has put large funds into post school industrial training through the Training Services Agencies of the Manpower Services Commission. Some of these funds have found their way into colleges of further education which have provided courses for the Training Services Agency. Much to the chagrin of local education authorities, these funds have been available only at the discretion of a para-governmental organization strong enough to impose its own demands on the education service and with a clear sense of its priorities, right or wrong. (Fenwick and McBride, 1981, p. 111)

There is, then, a sensitivity in the education service to the burgeoning role of the MSC. That 'chagrin' is too simple and pejorative a description is probably obvious, however, there is certainly an ambivalence toward the MSC of considerable proportion on the part of the 'official' providers of education. For example,

> ... there is the existence of the Manpower Services Commis-
> sion. It is perhaps prophetic that another paper in this report
> (Macfarlane in Context: Further Education's Response to MSC)
> is entitled *Education through MSC* rather than 'Education
> through MSC and the Local Authorities'. Will there be a time
> when another government agency will be given our job, a job
> that local authorities will apparently have failed to? (Horton,
> 1981, p. 339)

The ambivalence derives from an increasing appreciation that the MSC
is providing for a need which LEA's have not, in fact, been able to meet
within the traditional curriculum and examination framework. Nevertheless, an LEA has argued, 'it could be noted that in so far as training
and education can be artificially divided, education is the responsibility
of the LEA, not the Manpower Services Commission' (Avon LEA, FE
Sub-Committee, 30 March 1982, para. 9). Such a position is not likely
to be unusual on the part of LEAs, which in any case is a reflection of
their legal duties under the 1944 Act.

Therefore, notwithstanding some ambiguity and a certain ambivalence toward the field of 'training', any work deemed or interpreted to
be education is likely to be jealously guarded by the DES and LEAs.
The concepts of education and training have '... traditionally been
antithetical terms: education referring to the individual's personal
development, training to his professional development' (SCRACFE,
1980, p. 26, para. 8.1). However, the Standing Conference paper (*ibid.*)
argued sensibly that the working individual is a whole person and
cannot be divided into distinct educational and training parts. The
individual at work brings with him all his personal and professional
attributes, upon which his behaviour and performance in the job
depend.

> Education and training are not therefore opposed, or *necessarily*
> utterly distinct concepts, though at either extreme of the
> spectrum of experience relating the two may be found elements
> which appear to belong decisively within one or other category.
> (*ibid.*, p. 26)

It could be presumed, therefore, that the DES/LEAs see the work of
the MSC as being most appropriately confined to that narrow but
decisive extreme which is the training category.

The Standing Conference paper developed this argument and
concluded that the essentials of DES Circular 6/76 are pertinent, and

that the stress placed on the need for provision not to be related narrowly to the immediate job functions is sensible and appropriate. It also concluded, in similar vein to HMI (1980), that early specialization for pupils (before 16 years)

> ... could have the effect of directing pupils into a narrow stream before they have been able to accumulate sufficient knowledge to make objective decisions about themselves and their place in the social and economic framework. Overall pre-sixteen curriculum should be kept general and educational in intent: should provide especially basic core skills, encourage an alert interest in the world (including *appreciation* of working life), open access to a whole range of subjects and activities in an effort to develop and enhance the individual. (SCRACFE, *op. cit.*, p. 27)

There are, then, substantial views that vocational specialization should not occur in the pre-16 secondary school curriculum, and that job-specific training to the exclusion of education, in the sense of individual and personal development, is undesirable. Until recently this principle and the practice of comprehensive education had not been subject to any serious contrary action. The common curriculum, and the concept of minimum curricular differentiation, apparently sustained the notion of a liberal education for all and a practice of providing equal opportunity to all. Differentiation did occur but not until 16 when the top 60 per cent were carefully graded and the failures could leave and be mopped-up by the needs of industry for unskilled and semi-skilled labour. However, the New Training and Vocational Education Initiative (NTVEI) is clearly a serious challenge to the comprehensive and liberal common curriculum. Apart from the government's further powerful use of the specific grant through the MSC, the NTVEI gathers strength from the popular conception that education is somehow to blame for unemployment, and that this is to do with a lack of relevance, and that the NTVEI is obviously going to do something about it. The Secretary of State for Education, Sir Keith Joseph, seems to think the NTVEI will improve prospects for the bottom unexamined 40 per cent of the school leaving population. Michael Young (MSC Chairman), however, and perhaps more realistically '... wants to influence the whole curriculum, not just that of the least able. The NTVEI is the beach-head from which to colonise all secondary education' (*The Times Education Supplement*, 4 March 1983, editorial). Modernizing and making relevant the secondary curriculum for all seems to be one idea; making an alternative curriculum for the bottom 40 per cent, or shall we say the bottom half, seems to be *the* idea.

However, with the advent of mass youth unemployment, the question of relevance in the secondary school curriculum is fundamentally entangled with the question of what to do with 16-year-olds leaving and becoming unemployed, while at the same time having 'nothing to show' for their years at school. The relevance of their education has become inextricably bound up with their relevance to the labour market. By dint of a somewhat specious 'political' logic, the two kinds of relevance are treated as synonymous, hence stimulating a demand for a 'new curriculum' which is 'relevant' to the needs of these young people; their needs being apparently deemed coincident with the needs of 'industry', albeit industry has in fact little present need for them. However, as already argued, it is expected that the current deficiency of demand for labour will, at some presently indiscernible point, give way to an upturn, but an upturn characterized by a shifted structure.

The central effect, then, within the education system has been a dichotomization of the notion of relevance. In one half it applies to those young people who cannot get or hold jobs and who therefore manifestly need help, and help is equated with some form of training. In the other it applies to those 16-year-olds who cannot or do not seem likely to succeed in the traditional curriculum framework. It is likely, of course, that both halves are very substantially overlapped, perhaps almost one and the same in terms of identity. The MSC increasingly continues to initiate and 'provide' ad hoc curricula for those young people in the first half. The 'official' providers of education have largely questioned the framework of the curriculum they themselves provide, and have discussed an array of possible alternatives at stultifying length, while, in the meantime, the MSC has acted. There is a sense, an impression, of 'Rome burning' about the 'official' education system in this respect.

The fact that the first half of young people embraced by the MSC may be largely identical with the second half, the 'failers', is a serious dichotomy of another kind. This is to say, a potential dichotomy of provision. If, as now seems likely, the secondary system is to provide a 'new curriculum' for these 'halves', together with an examination framework (DES, May 1982, *op. cit.*), then MSC provision through the FE service and industry for leavers could become redundant in important respects, especially if (when) youth unemployment falls and declining rolls reach the tertiary sector. The secondary school and FE college system, under LEA/DES auspices, could provide an alternative to the MSC/YTS provision. This would assemble a kind of YTS curriculum in the secondary/tertiary education system as an aspect of full-time education.

There is something elephantine, but nevertheless inexorable as well, about the strategic lumbering for position on the part of the DES and LEAs. That their interests may well be compatible, even coincident, with those of the present government is very probable. This would be to recognize the government's need to evade the 'natural' extension of personal financial allowances to include all 16–19-year-olds, as well as grant-aided students in higher education. It needs to be presumed, of course, that the present scale of youth unemployment is merely a temporary aberration. In other words, the need to provide specifically for unemployed youth will become particular and small-scale instead of, as at present, general and large-scale. Need for such provision will be significantly reduced, in any case, if the 16-year-olds without qualification can be offered a further year in the 'official' education system; indeed, if in effect the school leaving age is raised to 17 years. This aspect of the 'new curriculum' and its inception are discussed in greater depth in later chapters. At this stage it is sufficient to recognize that the emergence of a 'new curriculum' has been importantly through the initiatives and accumulated experiences of the MSC, in the context of a moribund general education service over-weighed with its own debates and lack of resources. However,

> It is not supposed that LEAs will pass away. NTI is a national project that basically disregards the tier of local control of provision except for administrative purposes; it is concerned with educational sectors. The likelihood is, in a difficult financial climate, that the balance of power or control will swing even more firmly to the centre. In these circumstances, LEAs will more obviously be agents or providers of a national programme mainly decided elsewhere. (Small, 1983, p. 7)

In broad summary, a 'new curriculum' is emerging to replace the 'other' secondary school curriculum as a basis of education and qualification for the 'other half'. In some sense this 'new curriculum' can be seen as a new subject tacked to the range of HE defined subjects which form the official secondary school curriculum. However, its role as a subject among others is likely to be limited to the extent that it will form the whole curriculum for the 'other half'. At present access to this 'new curriculum' is confined to low attainment unemployed minimum age leavers, although it should be recognized that medium to high attainment leavers are now caught up in the unemployment net, and are likely to form a significant proportion of the catchment. However, to date, virtually no change has been introduced into the secondary school curriculum and its examination structure. In other words, the examination structure of the official curriculum continues to define it according to the needs of Higher Education, with CSEs and nothing at all providing for the 'other' curriculum. In the past few years MSC picked up a proportion of the bottom half as they left school and became unemployed. The MSC provided, through various agencies, of which the FE service was a major one, several schemes for coping with the youth unemployment problem. From such schemes (initiatives), mediated by such bodies as the FEU, a species of vocational preparation syllabus has emerged which has the form of a curriculum. This 'new curriculum' presently resides in a twilight world of institutional competition among official education provision, particular training instruments of national manpower policy, and general political imperatives for 'action' (doing something) to deal with the unemployment problem as it affects minimum age leavers. What the 'new curriculum' looks like is confined to various sightings from different viewpoints. From one position it is seen as a subject, examinable among others; from another position as a procedure for reducing youth unemployment; from another as a radical, new and relevant educational provision for the bottom half; from another as a means of restructuring the base of work-skills of the country's future manpower; from yet another viewpoint the 'new curriculum' is seen as a *curriculum* relevant to the needs of society and the individual.

Such differences of viewpoint are mounted on different perceptions of salient needs in our society. In each viewpoint, however, there is agreement that the future labour economy will be characterized by demand for a more broadly skilled workforce alongside a major demand-deficiency for unskilled workers. Through this common recognition there is agreement that major change in 16–19 and, indeed, the 14–19 curricular provision in our schools and colleges is needed. Precisely what that change should consist of is not established in practice or in theory as yet. Nevertheless, there are views and practices, indeed a plethora of such, which, it is generally presumed, will compose the 'new curriculum' in the event. Major initiatives are presently stirring the great educational and training pot in which a range of ingredients, known and unknown, are simmering. Several, perhaps too many, cooks are stirring the pot and trying to determine the recipe.

That determining the recipe is a matter of considerable importance in the long term cannot be doubted. It is clear, from the foregoing, that the 'new curriculum' is likely to be experienced by an increasing proportion of 16–19-year-olds, indeed to the extent that it may prove to be the most important 'subject' in the overall curriculum of the education system. But, such importance, perhaps, should not be confused with status.

> So far we have considered the definition, evaluation and distribution of elite education. But the curriculum of the schools for the masses that developed after the introduction of compulsory schooling in 1870 also requires consideration. This education, for the children of the 'labouring poor', was seen to be of fundamentally different kind, predominantly concerned with basic skills of numeracy and literacy, Though in content almost diametrically opposed to high-status education, the mass education curriculum may be analysed in similar ways. Unlike its counterpart it was defined and evaluated not by its consumers but by the same elite groups who defined high-status education. Its definition sprang from an appraisal of the knowledge regarded as appropriate for the new occupational roles of an industrial society. It was defined so that it did not present a challenge to the status of the knowledge on which elite curricula were based; rather it reinforced and re-emphasized the lower status of vocational and utilitarian knowledge and skills. . . .
>
> But the curriculum for the masses was called upon to serve for more urgent purposes than the provision of minimal skills. It was also required to facilitate social consensus. (Eggleston, 1977, p. 31)

Whatever else Eggleston is saying, this much is pertinent to the present time: large numbers of unoccupied and barely educated youths do not facilitate social consensus; and social dissent of this kind is difficult, if not impossible, to police forcefully and yet survive politically.

Treating curriculum as an organization in the terms of Chapter 1 suggests the 'new curriculum' will operate as a kind or type of organization in the secondary and tertiary education sectors with special links and new links to work behaviours drawn from industrial and service employment. The content of the 'new curriculum' will be controlled centrally by government through the MSC, and provided locally by LEAs and other institutions, some of which will be conglomerate in the fashion of groups of industrial and service organizations combining to supply 'new curriculum' organizations to the MSC. The institutional provision of the secondary school curriculum is in the process of major bifurcation. The DES and LEAs are becoming cast in the role of providers of an MSC centrally controlled range of technical and vocational curricula. The bifurcation reflects a division of curricular provision. In one half are pupils with 'academic' ability and professional and HE potential within a traditional but updated grammar curriculum leading to upward socio-economic mobility. The creation of a unified examination scheme for 16-year-olds will underwrite this updated curriculum. In the other half are pupils of low 'academic' ability provided with an alternative examination system controlled by the MSC to top out a utilitarian technical and vocational 'new curriculum', leading to the work of the 'new labourer'. The institutional bifurcation reflects the new curricular bifurcation at 14 years for pupils. 'New curriculum' organizations will be characterized by major centralized control, utilitarian purpose, and low status. They will operate in the context of labour market analyses or speculations unable to predict with any certainty what precisely 'new curriculum' organizations should do as instruments of a somewhat opaque national manpower policy. Consequently, the influence of vocational training analysts such as the Institute of Manpower Studies, the FEU, industrial institutions, together with political predilections, will be of key significance to the central power, the MSC.

3   The New Training Initiative: Jungle Clearance or More Growth?

Education about the labour market and its changing face could be an essential feature of all future curricula, although the effects which this knowledge have on individual career planning remain debateable. The paths through the jungle are unlikely to become much more simple, but if the continued contact between schools, colleges, employers and training boards has the effect of reducing the gap between education and training, and producing young people who are prepared in every sense for their future working life, then the paths will at least lead to a satisfactory destination. To describe these paths as a maze implies that prior planning has taken place; that FE is an intentional puzzle, and that it has a single conclusion. The variety of provision will ensure that it remains a jungle; but with some intelligent planting, and some clearing of the thickets, the jungle may become more easily penetrated, and the clearings which exist in it may become more accessible to each other.

FEU, Jan. 1981, p. 47

The purpose of this chapter is to identify, describe and analyze a 'new curriculum' apparently rising from the ashes of heated political debate about youth unemployment. The chapter takes as its starting point the Conservative government's December 1981 White Paper, *A New Training Initiative: A Programme for Action*, Cmnd 8455, referred to hereafter as *NTI* (Dec. 1981, Govt). The White Paper, while not a pivotal document in itself, is of central importance to the English education system and, in particular to the further education sector. This, and the emergence of other New Training Initiative documents is used here as a way of identifying the 'new curriculum'. Essentially, the term 'new curriculum' is related to the burgeoning of post-16 courses, available, at least, to those who cannot find employment, which introduce a major new element into the present range of curricula available to the 16–19 age group, and for which no academic qualifications for entry are applicable, and for which a personal 'allowance' will be available to participants, and that these developments may substantially influence the pre-16 secondary school curriculum.

As indicated in Chapters 1 and 2, the socio-economic, political and educational 'context' in which the 'new curriculum' resides is complex. At this point it is important to identify, so far as possible, what is in fact likely to be resident in that context; in other words, what the key features of 'new curriculum' organizations are likely to be. Such identification would, for example, make possible the proper analysis of relationships between the 'new curriculum' and its context. In this respect it is worth emphasizing that, while contextuals (that is, contextual factors) impinge on and affect this curriculum in various ways, the fact is that 'something' *will* be taught to someone irrespective of, or because of, the effects of such contextuals. This 'something' will involve teachers and learners in curriculum organizations, and these organizations, good, bad or indifferent, whether congruent or incongruent with socio-economic aims, educational aims, political purposes, and so on, may exist in very large numbers and share common characteristics of sufficient scale and significance to warrant their identification as a significant 'new curriculum' in the English education system. The purpose of this chapter is to identify what the 'something' is most likely to be, not necessarily what it *ought* to be. The term 'curriculum' is used here in the terms of Chapter 1, as comprised of organizations, and in this sense it includes the key features of the entire process which their members experience. Discussion of curriculum definition and principles of curriculum design was developed in Chapter 1, and in Chapter 2, in relation to certain broad contextuals. It was crucially taken to include some aspects normally treated as external to curriculum, but which actually regularize the experience of students. Such inclusions came within the terms of the Chapter 1 view that a curriculum is importantly comprised of actual curriculum organizations, and therefore behaves in ways common to organizations.

While the *NTI* (Dec. 1981, Govt) is a document central to this discussion, it is important to note that there were two *NTIs* originally in circulation. There was the already mentioned *NTI* (Dec. 1981, Govt), and as well *A New Training Initiative: An Agenda for Action,* published by the Manpower Services Commission (MSC) on the same day, and hereafter referred to as *NTI* (Dec. 1981, MSC). This derived from the MSC's consultative document of May 1981, *A New Training Initiative*, hereafter referred to as *NTI* (May 1981, MSC). Needless to say, the debate about 'the' NTI (unspecified) has often been confusing because of this peculiar synonymity between proposals vying for command of 'the initiative'.

For the purposes of this chapter, reference to either NTI is restricted to proposals broadly affecting the 16–19 age group. The three objectives are quoted in full, below, from which it can be seen that objectives (i) and (ii) affect more directly this age group, while objective (iii) is to do with adults (although by natural process it could come to affect them).

(i)   we must develop skill training including apprenticeship in such a way as to enable young people entering at different ages and with different educational attainments to acquire agreed standards of skill appropriate to the jobs available and to provide them with a basis for progression through further learning;

(ii)   we must move towards a position where all young people under the age of eighteen have the opportunity either of continuing in full-time education or of entering a period of planned work experience combined with work-related training and education;

(iii)   we must open up widespread opportunities for adults, whether employed, unemployed or returning to work, to acquire, increase or update their skills and knowledge during the course of their working lives. (*NTI*, Dec. 1981, Govt, p. 3; *NTI*, Dec. 1981, MSC, para. 3)

The government's proposals were largely subsumed under heads to do with a Youth Training Scheme (YTS), which is the first point of a ten-point programme for action,

(i)   a new £1 billion a year Youth Training Scheme, guaranteeing from September 1983 a full year's foundation training for all those leaving school at the minimum age without jobs; (*NTI*, Dec. 1981, Govt, para. 3)

It is to this full year of foundation training, and what students will experience in the organization of that period (the 'new curriculum'), that this chapter is addressed.

Use of the word 'curriculum' as an organization is illustrated by an early difference between the government's initiative and the MSC's in respect of youth training, subsequently resolved (20 June 1982) on the matter of the rate and conditions of 'allowance' for NTI (unspecified) trainees. In the scope of the use of the term 'curriculum' is included the matter of 'allowances' as being a feature of the entire process a student experiences through being a member of the curriculum organization. The *NTI* (Dec. 1981, Govt), on training allowances and benefit arrangements, starts out by saying, 'The new scheme is first and last a training scheme' (para. 34). It goes on to propose, in effect, that 'trainees' would contribute to the cost of their training by way of the level of their allowance. This assumed that the YTS would be reserved for only those minimum school leaving age leavers who were without jobs. Minimum school leaving age leavers, entitled under the government's proposals to enter a YTS, would receive a training allowance of £15 per week, which effectively meant they would contribute £10 per week to their own training cost, assuming the MSC proposed level of allowance as under YOP of £25 (plus) per week. Those not choosing to enter a YTS were to be debarred from receiving supplementary benefit, and would in this sense be subject to a financial 'encouragement'. This 'coercive' aspect of the government's proposals was the subject of considerable controversy, and led to agreement that the allowance will be £25 (plus) per week, without the supplementary benefit 'encouragement' being applied.

The 'new curriculum' will carry in it, then, an experience of financial independence and, for the first time for the leavers, freedom from direct compulsion. It has to be said, of course, that their choice is presently mainly between YTS and simple unemployment. Although this cannot be taken as a wide choice, it is nevertheless a choice of sorts which the leaver will have to make. So far as it goes, in this respect, the 'new curriculum' will not be compulsory in the way 'school' was. No matter how much subject choice (theoretical or actual) a pupil had been given while at school, he was legally obliged to attend and do what the school told him to do.

Certainly, there is close agreement between the government's proposals and the MSC's that the new YTS should be very much a *training* scheme and be heavily oriented to preparation for work. It is in this sense vocational, although most participants may not have a realizable vocation when they start out.

It [YTS] will aim to equip unemployed young people to adapt successfully to the demands of employment; to have a fuller appreciation of the world of industry, business and technology in which they will be working; and to develop basic and recognised skills which employers will require in the future. (*NTI*, Dec. 1981, Govt, para. 24)

And, in relation to standards, 'In our view, standards need to be based firmly on the skills, knowledge and experience actually required in the performance of a job or range of jobs' (*NTI*, Dec. 1981, MSC, para.21). Both *NTIs* were agreed that the 'new curriculum' would be one of training and not education, and that the training is for work. In this sense the term 'curriculum' survives as a synonym for 'syllabus', as the Department of Employment *Glossary of Training Terms* interestingly points out:

SYLLABUS: A statement of the subject matter (content) of a training course or part of it. It may indicate the time to be devoted to each part of the training but not usually the order in which items should be learnt nor the methods of instruction to be used. The word 'curriculum' is sometimes used as a synonym for syllabus. (Department of Employment, *Glossary of Training Terms*, p. 27)

The political significance of the distinction between training and education, and the relative spheres of influence and power between the DES and MSC, is of obvious importance. There is little doubt that training is the domain of the MSC; and the YTS, whatever it turns out to be in the end, will in this respect certainly remain a *training* scheme, with all that word implies in terms of who will be in control. At this point it is sufficient to recognize that the 'new curriculum' is presently, and is likely to remain, training in the control of the MSC and, therefore, more significantly, in the sphere of influence of the Department of Employment rather than the DES (and LEAs). This point is probably not at issue; however, the prospect of a vocational curriculum, under the central aegis of the MSC, which through an institutional metamorphosis becomes a school and college curriculum remaining under this central aegis, is certainly at issue.

In spite of a considerable volume of reports and papers from the MSC, including government statements, not much has been said about the curriculum itself. However, within education considerable documentation has built up about curricular issues to do with the 16–19 age group. This ranges from Schools Council work, to reports of the HMI, the work of the Assessment of Performance Unit (APU), professional associations, educationalists, the DES and LEAs. Much of this work is to do with the major issues of secondary and further education and the problems of examination, standards, subject comprehensiveness, equality of opportunity, and so on. In an important sense it is undesirable to separate curriculum issues to do with leavers of minimum school leaving age and YTS from the broader issues of, for example, GCE O- and A-level, CSE, the old Q and F and then N and F, I-level, and now GCSE, examination discussions, together with the whole gamut of vocational FE curricula.

However, at this stage, there is considerable advantage in avoiding the compound introduction of these wider issues. It is a major point here that so little has in fact been said directly by the MSC about the curriculum (syllabus) for the new YTS; although various bodies have produced intensive studies of foundation training for 16–19s, notably the Further Education Curriculum Review and Development Unit (FEU), the Association of Colleges in Further and Higher Education (ACFHE), the Standing Conference of Regional Advisory Councils for Further Education (SCRACFE), National Foundation for Educational Research (NFER), City and Guilds of London Institute (CGLI), the Royal Society of Arts (RSA), and the Institute of Manpower Studies (IMS) – for the MSC. Other work, too, has been done by the Further Education Staff College (Coombe Lodge), together with a considerable number of individual studies published in academic and training journals. Nevertheless, analysis of what government and/or the MSC have said on this shows a remarkable lack of detailed direction. There was no obvious direct reference by government or the MSC to any of this major work being taken as authoritative. Certainly, it was indicated that such work made a valuable contribution, but there was no clear direction that the work of a particular institution was to form the YTS curriculum/syllabus before the MSC and FEU formal joint statement about curricular design and implementation late in 1982. Of course, as discussed later, intimations of FEU influence in that respect have been thick on the ground ever since the NTI was announced.

An overall review shows that much of the work done by such bodies refers significantly to foundation training involving further education in terms of *education* and training, and not simply in terms of 'Further Education' being a sector for the part supply of a *training* course specified by the government and/or MSC. The Youth Opportunities Programme (YOP) and other MSC youth schemes are referred to, most notably YOP and Unified Vocational Preparation (UVP). With regard to YOP it is tacitly recognized by government, the MSC and others that there have been major weaknesses in the programme, which have led to public criticisms of various kinds, with the end result that the credibility of the programme was undermined. The *NTI* (Dec. 1981, Govt) gave a clear indication that YOP was no longer adequate in scale and quality.

> The young unemployed will remain a priority group in terms of new training arrangements. The Youth Opportunities Programme was introduced in 1978 especially to help the minority of young people who were unemployed and quite unprepared or ill equipped for working life by means of a relatively short period of work experience or work preparation. Since then it has become clear that we need a full-scale training programme that provides for an increasing number and range of unemployed young people, and the Youth Opportunities Programme has begun to develop in this direction. The Government now proposes that a new and better youth training scheme should be introduced by the Commission to cover all unemployed minimum age school-leavers by September 1983. (*NTI*, Dec. 1981, Govt, para. 23)

It is clear, then, that MSC and government intend YTS to develop from YOP *and* UVP experience.

In effect the clearest direction initially given for the 'new curriculum' by the MSC or government was the general statement on training content in the *NTI* (Dec. 1981, Govt). In this the aims of YTS are heavily oriented to work preparation. The general aims are to be achieved by courses designed to effectively integrate skills, knowledge and experience through planned and supervised work experience, with opportunities for off-the-job training or further education, and should take account of a range of abilities and learning aptitudes, together with local labour market characteristics. There should be five main elements to the course: *induction and assessment*; *basic skills*; *occupationally relevant education and training*; *guidance and counselling*; *record and review of progress*. It can be seen, immediately, that any question of a broader curriculum to include say students' interests outside a putative or ostensive 'vocation' was thoroughly constrained. 'Education' was squeezed out and a sort of nineteenth century elementary technical school course squeezed in, wrapped, of course, in glosses to do with the interest of the trainees in getting an occupation. Personal and life skills were not specifically referred to in the government's White Paper, although almost always effectively included in YOP and UVP courses.

What is clear is that considerable MSC effort has gone into

exploring how a YTS could be delivered on a national scale for some 300,000 young people in 1983–84 and 1984–85, in terms of a £1 billion budget. As a result there has been a great concentration of response about the organization of the scheme and its funding arrangements. The 'politics' of proposals and responses, although often subdued and subtle, are always determined, because much sectional interest is at stake for general and individual institutions within the education system and the private sector. This compounds and complicates the wider political aspirations of left and right in British politics, in so far as they are inextricably bound up with the stances of many educational interest groups. Consequently, while considerable curriculum debate has taken place outside, or on the periphery of, the central debate between MSC and government on the 'new curriculum', little curriculum debate has actually occurred in the main arena itself. An important subsequent shift has been the subtle but deliberate extension of the YTS from generating training only organizations, as in the *NTI* (Dec. 1981, Govt), to training and education organizations by the MSC's Youth Task Group in its report of April 1982.

   This report is important in several respects. It was influential, for example, in persuading government not to maintain its coercive stance toward training allowances and supplementary benefits. But it is the subtle inclusion of broader principles in the 'new curriculum' than were in the main statement in *NTI* (Dec. 1981, Govt) that is most significant. In the guise of general flexibility, the Youth Task Group Report (April 1982, paras. 4.9 and 4.10) referred to a YTS which is to 'provide a foundation *both* for work and for further training as appropriate' (para. 4.9, my emphasis). The reference to 'further training' becomes provision within the YTS of 'relevant education' (para 4.10), and to 'be able, at completion of the programme, to transfer his or her acquired skills, knowledge and experience to other employment contexts, including further skills, training or education' (MSC, *Youth Task Group Report*, April 1982, para. 4.10 i). There is also reference to 'personal and life skills' (para. 4.10 g). There is little doubt that the YTS, in terms of its aim to equip young people for work, may also be, in terms of the Task Group Report, looking to equip young people for more education (and training). There are, of course, good socio-economic and political reasons for such extension, which might partly explain why the government accepted the Youth Task Group Report. However, in educational terms there is clearly a curriculum development involved of larger scope than originally envisaged by the *NTI* (Dec. 1981, Govt).

   Essentially, then, a basic framework of objectives for the YTS 'new curriculum' was initially established by the government through the Department of Employment (DOE) and MSC, involving only peripherally the DES, and expressed in *NTI* (Dec. 1981, Govt). In the simplest terms the 'new curriculum' can be described in terms of four questions: *who?*; *how?*; *what?*; *why?* Using this format the *NTI* (Dec. 1981, Govt) 'new curriculum' can be described, and then compared with that of the MSC Youth Task Group Report of April 82.

Figure 1 provides a schematic representation of the original *NTI* (Dec. 1981, Govt) 'new curriculum'. From this can be seen its explicit proposed process. There are obvious and less obvious non-educational aims for this YTS which will be identified and discussed more fully later. The immediately apparent major characteristic is the specificity of its aim or object: to prepare unemployed minimum age school leavers for employment. With its original coercive aspect, *i.e.* the applicability and level of training allowance and supplementary benefit, this YTS effectively raised the minimum school leaving age for those without jobs to 17 years. The labour market assumption underlying this, and the curriculum itself, was that these young people would be better able to find jobs after one year of preparation on two counts. First, the market would be permanently deficient of a complete year of job demand from leavers (without jobs), which should effectively improve the supply/demand ratio for young labour in the market. This would defer supply, for the duration of the YTS programmes, of one annual cohort of minimum age school leavers who could not find jobs. This would be an obvious anomaly except for the interpretation of the second count, which is that those young people who had completed their YTS would out-compete for jobs those minimum age leavers who had not. In other words, YTS leavers would be generally more attractive to employers than minimum school age leavers without such training.

In this way the scheme as a whole (its duration as a scheme) will last as long as it is required, having implanted in it the seeds of its own dissolution, providing it is restricted to recruiting only minimum age school leavers who are without jobs. Dissolution depends on an upturn in demand for young workers, which can be assisted by making them ready trained, and by eroding their wage expectations and union influence over this. It also relates to the trend of downturn in supply from 1984 through the 1990s (Census and DES Report No. 99, May 1982), otherwise known as declining rolls.

The syllabus/curriculum, too, would be very much under the control of the MSC, in terms of the MSC's grip on the organizational

Figure 1. Schematic Presentation of the NTI (Dec. 1981, Govt) YTS 'New Curriculum'

Who	*How*	*What*	*Why*
Young unemployed, specifically: minimum age leavers without jobs, provided with financial incentive to take up YTS place offer through training allowance at £15.00 (lower than present YOPS allowances at £25.00) and subject to disallowance of supplementary benefit if offer refused.	Through YTSs delivered by the MSC through private companies careers service FE (LEAs) and the involvement of sponsors and managing agencies at local level.	A one-year programme consisting of: induction and assessment; basic skills; occupationally relevant education and training, both on and off-the-job; guidance and counselling, recording and review of progress against 'agreed' standards.	To enable participants to: 1 adapt successfully to demands of employment; 2 have a fuller appreciation of the world of industry, business and technology in which they will be working; 3 develop basic and recognized skills which employers will require in the future.
Characteristics 1 Partially coercive 2 Limited mixed ability range 3 Narrow and specific range of access in 16–19 age group: specifically limited to unemployed 16-year-olds	*Characteristics* 1 Major control held by MSC	*Characteristics* 1 Generalized Content 2 Implies complex organization and heavy administration 3 Maximum duration one year	*Characteristics* 1 Specifically vocational to extent of training for at least specific job family 2 No progression in explicit terms

and funding aspects of the delivery of YTSs throughout the country. Great attention was paid to this by the MSC in the *NTI* (Dec. 1981, MSC), and the government in its *NTI* (Dec. 1981, Govt). Indeed, the government was quite explicit:

> We therefore set out in this White Paper our decisions on immediate action and proposals for the longer term. These draw substantially upon the recommendations made by the Commission in its report and the Commission will play a central role in their implementation. (*NTI*, Dec. 1981, Govt. para. 2)

The persistent initial emphasis on the 'new curriculum' being to do with training confirmed government's intention to implement and develop it under the specific auspices of the MSC, and not through the official education system of DES/LEAs.

Nevertheless, the *NTI* (Dec. 1981, Govt) did open up investigation of the prospects for extending YTS to cover employed as well as unemployed young people, within available resources (para. 3 iv). It established the already mentioned MSC Youth Task Group to report by April 1982. This report (MSC, April 1982) modified the 'new curriculum' in the several important respects outlined above. The Figure 1 scheme was, therefore, effectively modified by the Task Group Report in the following ways, illustrated in Figure 2. The 'who' was extended to approximate a little closer to the ultimate NTI object of the MSC and government, which is to enable all young people below the age of 18, not continuing in full-time education, to have the opportunity of entering training, or a period of planned work experience. So far this means a YTS, but the New Training and Vocational Education Initiative (NTVEI) is a clearly related long-term strategy for dissociating such training from unemployment and the concomitant of personal allowances for participants. The Task Group recommended that by September 1983 YTSs should provide opportunities for all 16-year-olds who have left full-time education for work, together with those 17-year-olds leaving full-time education and who become unemployed (para. 4.6). This significantly broadened the basis for recruitment. Taken together with the relaxation on allowances and supplementary benefit, the 'who' in the catchment was changed in four respects. They will be voluntarily involved in the YTS; they will not necessarily be unable to find jobs; they will be likely to provide a wider range of abilities in the scheme; and unemployed 17-year-olds are to be in the scope of the scheme.

Figure 2. Schematic Presentation of the MSC Youth Task Group (April 1982) YTS 'New Curriculum'

Who	How	What	Why
Changed cf. Figure 1	Same cf. Figure 1	Changed cf. Figure 1	Changed cf. Figure 1
Employed or unemployed young people 16–17 years old, specifically: minimum age school leavers with or without jobs. YOP level training allowance and no disallowance of supplementary benefit for those not taking up training offers. Moves towards providing training opportunity for all young people below 18 years.		A programme of foundation training for work or further training, normally one year duration but open to reduction or extension of time in relation to needs of each participant. The programme should meet the following MSC criteria: proper induction and assessment; minimum of three months off-the-job training or relevant FE, defined core skills; work experience; training in skills relevant to a family or related occupations; process skills; personal and life skills; counselling; records of achievement against promulgated standards. Reference is made to IMS and FEU work.	To enable participants to: transfer acquired skills, knowledge and experience to other employment contexts, including further skills training or education.
Characteristics 1 Voluntary 2 Extended (mixed) ability range 3 Wider access in 16–19 group, now includes all 16-year-olds plus 17-year-olds without jobs.		*Characteristics* 1 More specific, establishes principle of criteria. For standards, reference to IMS and FEU 2 Continues to imply complex organization and heavy administration 3 Duration can exceed one year.	*Characteristics* 1 Very specifically vocational 2 Open for progression to further training or education

The '*how*' retains its original main characteristic of control being very much retained by the MSC. The '*what*' reflects the subtle change in emphasis toward education as well as training by extension of the '*why*', which is to include preparation not only for work but also for continued training or relevant further education. The '*what*' becomes less generalized, but certainly continues to imply complex course organization and heavy administration. From Figure 2 it can be seen that the '*what*' of the one-year (or more) programme is less generalized. Specifically, the work of the Institute of Manpower Studies (IMS) and the FEU is referred to by the Youth Task Group (para. 4.10 e). It is in respect of this work that extrapolation can be undertaken in order to identify the YTS 'new curriculum' in more detail. Of course, some LEAs and/or individual institutions could subject themselves to efforts to 'reinvent the wheel', as 'original' duplication is sometimes called. However, with the MSC effectively in control, the Figure 2 'curriculum' will prevail as the substantive framework, with IMS and FEU work providing a body of detail. Consequently, the 'new curriculum' can be more fully identified and described by analysis of the IMS and FEU work, in relation to the MSC Youth Task Group framework.

In respect of the work of the FEU it should be at once recognized that its key strategic interest is in the question of linkage between training and education, that is, between initial, or pre-vocational preparation training, and progression from that to further training and education. Its early work on 16-19 educational and training provision, *Signposts* (Jan. 1981), *Vocational Preparation* (Jan. 1981) and *A Basis for Choice* (Jan. 1979), demonstrates this major concern. In the simplest terms, the concern is to ensure that 16–19 curricula are usefully available as a range of choices for all 16-year-olds, and that, in particular, foundation training is an aspect of that range of choice, while not necessarily being an end in itself, but providing a means for participants to progress either to employment or to further education and training or both. Importantly associated with this broad concern is the FEU's extension of the concept of relevance. The government and MSC's original notion of relevance seemed restricted to the provision of training which was relevant to a national manpower policy, that is, to jobs. The FEU developed its concept of a negotiated 'bespoke' vocational preparation course (FEU, Jan. 1981, para. 30) which, through negotiated 'contracts' with participants, would relate further learning to the experience of individual participants.

For most people, learning is effective if it is seen to be RELEVANT. For many young people RELEVANCE is related to EXPERIENCE, which may mean work or other real-life situations. A preferred vocational focus, even if ephemeral or vicarious, often produces the necessary motivation for further learning. (FEU, June 1982, p. 2, para. iv)

It can be understood, then, that the developments in the YTS introduced by the Youth Task Group Report (MSC, April 1982) provided an important connection between this strategic interest of the FEU and the development of the 'new curriculum'. The early direction of the FEU in this respect can be found in its paper, 'Progressing from Vocational Preparation – A Discussion of Issues' (FEU, Dec. 1981). The paper has as its primary aim:

To emphasise that if vocational preparation is to become a central educational process, available to all young people whether or not they are involved in other study or training, then it must be recognized as such. Thus if NTI is to be a vehicle for a long overdue provision, then its design-base must allow and encourage progression to more advanced education and/or training by a wider range of school leavers than has hitherto been possible. This will mean as we explain below, not only new attitudes towards selection and assessment, changed concepts of skill and competence, different ways of defining access and success, but probably a radical re-appraisal of many of our more 'advanced' education and training courses. (FEU, Dec. 1981, para. 5)

It can be seen, at once, that this is a substantially broader aim than that of the MSC or government. Apart from the difficulty of a radical reappraisal of, or in the event actually radically changing, advanced education, in terms of ensuring vocational preparation has something 'higher' to progress to, there is the central difficulty of determining what, in any case, vocational preparation should itself be doing. If it has the limited aims of the *whys* in Figure 1 then progression is assuredly not designed. However, and this is the significance of the Youth Task Group Report, if the aims of the *whys* in Figure 2 prevail, then the ground is laid for the seeds of major change to be sown by the FEU through its curriculum proposals for vocational preparation. Because government accepted the Youth Task Group Report, these wider FEU curriculum proposals remain firmly on the general agenda.

Figure 3 presents the main dimensions of the 'new curriculum', as

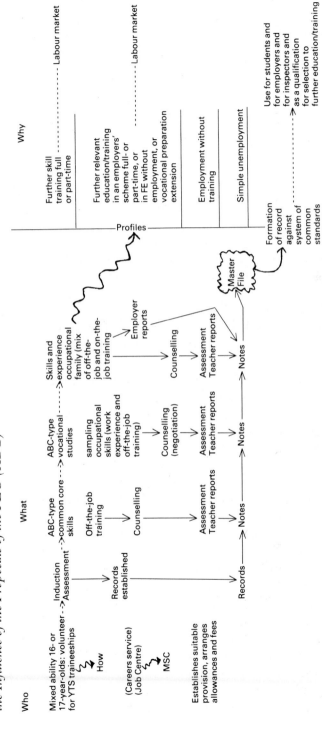

Figure 3.   Schematic Presentation of the 'New Curriculum' in Terms of the Individual Participant, and Taking into Account the Influence of the Proposals of the FEU (ABC)

influenced by the FEU, established to achieve the aims in Figure 2. It can be seen that the FEU influenced syllabus/curriculum takes serious account of the personal development of the trainee, in a framework of occupationally oriented learning, which can lead to progression from this YTS 'new curriculum' to other curricula, as well as specific employment. The internal process (the *what*) of the curriculum is essentially derived from the FEU model, reproduced here as Figure 4 (FEU, Dec. 1982, para. 14). What is most striking about the development is that it highlights the considerable scale of administration required simply to generate sufficient information on the progress of each trainee to make the formation of an intelligible and genuinely significant record of achievement feasible. The basic question of its desirability will be discussed later. These records and their administration do not take into account other aspects of substantial administration and management implied by the 'new curriculum', for example, the management of providing work experience relevant to each trainee.

A review of previous FEU work in the area of vocational preparation, notably *A Basis For Choice* (June 1979), *Vocational Preparation* (Jan. 1981) and *ABC in Action* (Sept. 1981), shows that the general position of the FEU is based on a development and synthesis of this previous work. The components of the Figure 3 model can be described in considerable detail using this base of previous work. The IMS's recent review and collation of issues in foundation or vocational training for the MSC, *Foundation Training Issues* (IMS, Feb. 1982), is an additional and complementary source of information, giving significant indication of trends of opinion and analysis as to what the YTS 'new curriculum' should consist of. It is necessary to recognize that a plethora of additional papers, booklets, checklists, guidance, opinions and such like exist which are either directly or indirectly to do with the development of the 'new curriculum'. However, the main synthesizing agencies are the FEU and the MSC, with the work of the IMS counting as work of the MSC. It is with reference, then, to the work of the FEU and the MSC that the following detailed descriptive exposition of the 'new curriculum' is made, Figure 3 providing the general framework.

Mention should at once be made of the substantial reference both the FEU and MSC have made to the experience of YOP, UVP, CGLI foundation courses, RSA basic courses, and FE college-based pre-employment courses. Both the IMS and FEU are broadly agreed on the deficiencies of some of these schemes, and on their value as an experience base for the development of YTS.

The existing modes of provision have their own strengths and weaknesses: many YOP programmes are weak on basic skills and the work experiences are not always easy to monitor; UVP schemes are invariably too short; college-based courses rarely provide sufficient work experience. Inter-agency co-operation could provide a more efficient and equitable vocational preparation process, based on agreed national curricular criteria, but tailored to meet the needs of each young person in the light of local employment prospects. (FEU, Circular on Vocational Preparation, March 1981, para. 4)

And, in respect of YOP:

The majority of young people in YOP spend their time with an employer. Until recently the overwhelming majority of employers have been small, often with little tradition of training. Because the young people are untrained and training is minimal, the work they can be given demands few occupational skills and at the end of the period such young people emerge with little to show except some important world of work skills. Moreover, many young people are not given experience in more than one type of work, particularly in places where the YOP trainee is being substituted for a properly employed person. Hence the widespread reaction by young people that YOP offers no training of lasting value and that without a job at the end it is a 'con'. (IMS, Feb. 1982, para. 2.2.25)

It must be stressed that both the IMS and FEU consider blanket criticism of the quality of YOPS (and UVP) unfair, but recognize that wide variations in the *quality* of training provided is derived from,

. . . a characteristic of YOP that learning objectives, content and method have been defined in the loosest possible terms leaving each sponsor virtually free to do what he likes. This has inevitably meant that standards are equally variable, and so are all other quality hallmarks. The first question to be answered is, therefore, whether learning objectives should be more closely defined.' (IMS, Feb. 1982, para. 2.2.21)

There is now general agreement that learning objectives should be closely defined. This is either a stated view, as in the case of the FEU, or implicit in the general presentation of issues, as in the case of IMS. Indeed, there developed a definite consensus among the many parties involved that the YTS should have closely defined learning objectives. This is inevitable if, as seems to be the case, trainee achievement is to be measured against standards in order to achieve 'quality' training within the scheme. Consequently, the amalgam of FEU and MSC (IMS) and government views on the learning objectives and content of the 'new curriculum' provides the basis for a detailed identification and description of it.

At this point a detailed extension of the Chapter 1 discussion of the notion of curriculum as organizations could appear useful. However, in keeping with the general strategy of the book, it is preferable to concentrate at this point in conventional terms on the emergence of the 'new curriculum', its identification and description, deferring analysis of probable merits or demerits in terms of behaviour as organizations.

Essentially the MSC will send trainees to YTS provider organizations called 'managing agencies'. Such agencies will be responsible for delivering the 'new curriculum' to the trainees. Provider organizations can be private training companies, private companies with training facilities, LEAs, public corporations or authorities or groups of these in partnership. It is envisaged that such provider organizations will be assessed by the MSC's new Area Manpower Boards as providing 'quality' YTSs. The providers will, therefore, be the main instruments of supply of the 'new curriculum' for trainees rather than the MSC itself. The curriculum they provide will be constructed along the lines of Figure 3 (accommodating Figure 4), described here in terms of the process to be experienced by the trainees. The process can be divided into six aspects: induction; common core skills; sampling occupational skills; skills development and experience in a chosen occupational family; assessment and progression; a counselling and recording process throughout the course. The following descriptions are adduced for each of these from FEU and MSC work.

On *induction*, although referred to as important, there is little direct instruction as to precisely what a provider should do to properly induct trainees. Nevertheless, there are many references to general practices widely used in predecessor schemes and in other courses. The inference is that the trainee should receive both group and individual induction. This should comprise the normal mechanics of ice-breaking between staff and trainees and trainees and trainees, with detailing of basic rules of behaviour and information about organizational facilities, and an introduction to the course. Individual induction seems mainly to involve finding out the interests, experience and probable capacities of individual trainees, in order to provide an information base to guide decisions about subsequent orientation of the course for the individual. It also *seems* inevitable that it should provide a base of information about the individual trainee's attainments/capabilities on starting the course as a standard against which his individual progress can be measured throughout, and especially upon completion or leaving.

Induction in this respect could become heavily oriented to assessment. While there is considerable intimation of profiling as the means of providing leaving 'certification', there is virtually nothing directly stated about entry profiles. This is a surprising gap in material to date about the 'new curriculum'. In any case, an induction and assessment period of two to four weeks seems likely to be allocated, and in theory could involve considerable testing of various sorts. Such testing could include checks on general attainment and specific skills, together with tutor opinion about a trainee's general attributes. Obviously, a common format between YTS 'new curriculum' organizations for measures and attributes would be required, especially if it were assumed that the induction assessment process was to provide an adequate means of comparing the performance of the trainee on entering to that on leaving, as well as introducing the course and encouraging active participation. However, such an assumption is somewhat large, and it seems most unlikely that measuring a trainee's real or actual progress will be seen as having 'practical' value by the MSC. Presumably, that is a reflection of the degree to which output, summative measurements against 'recognizable standards' will be a dominant feature of the 'new curriculum'. Formative assessment throughout would be 'informative' for the summation/certificate. If such formative assessment is to be formative, as well as an administrative records system, then entry profiles of trainees would seem useful, in spite of their redundancy to a criterion referenced attainment profile set against pass/fail 'standards'. In any case, it is very apparent that a great deal of administrative effort will have to go into the formation of trainees' records from the moment they start their courses.

After the process of induction and assessment, trainees enter a period of ABC-type common core skills training, sometimes confusingly called 'basic skills training'. The movement of the trainees from induction and assessment to the common core skills training is seen by the FEU to be continuous in the trainees' experience and not a stepped change from a first part or 'bit' of the course to a second 'bit'. Indeed, the course should not be a series of steps or parts, but a continuous flow. Therefore, unless there are sufficient numbers of trainees to 'stream', mixed attainment (and ability?) groups may enter the common core skills phase. Consequently, teaching would need to be geared as mixed ability teaching to ensure each trainee progresses from his particular attainment level at a pace suited to his ability.

The FEU (June 1979), in a major collation of pre-employment training practices, suggested that the common core should consist of the introduction to the college, together with the induction and assessment phase and introduction to various sectors of employment, with the opportunity to sample different work tasks. It went on to say,

> The core as a whole should provide opportunities for the young people to develop
> - practical numeracy
> - their ability to communicate
> - their ability to learn from study, experience and colleagues
> - social skills and understanding to a variety of contexts
> - self confidence, self awareness and adaptability
> - a variety of manipulative and physical skills
> - their awareness of various technological, environmental, political, economic and aesthetic factors which affect their lives
> - a basis from which to make informed and realistic career choices and it should do this in this [sic] context of their intention to enter the world of work in the near future. (FEU, June 1979, para. 57)

In conjunction with this it is worth quoting the *NTI* (Dec. 1981, Govt) White Paper, which indicates a narrow concept of basic skills:

> *Basic Skills.* The programme will aim to ensure that basic skills like numeracy and literacy have been acquired; to develop some practical competence in the use of tools and machinery and in some basic operations, and to foster skills in communication (in interview for example). (*NTI*, Dec. 1981, Govt, para. 26)

It can be seen from Figure 3 that common core skills is envisaged as a deliberate phase. Consequently, the induction and assessment, while continuous, form a deliberate diagnostic process leading to the common core skills phase. It can also be seen that the 'intention to enter the world of work in the near future' is extended to include relevant further training and/or education as an alternative to immediate employment. Consequently, trainees will need to explore skills of learning associated with more advanced course work, as well as skills solely associated with work as such. The initial divergence of view between the FEU concept of common core skills, or rather basic skills, and the government's (and, indeed, many employers') has widened considerably. However, the government, through the MSC, seems to have tacitly accepted the FEU's 'changing concept of skill' (FEU, Nov. 1982, pp. 1 ff). In this the FEU pointed out that the notion of skills limited to performing a manipulative occupational task leads to the misconception that they are only to do with the visible characteristics of job specific skills.

> The term skill includes not only the industrial connotation of a skilled worker but also a psychological perspective. The psychological use of the term skill is that skilled performance requires perception, decision making, knowledge, judgement and understanding, and at the same time all skills involve some kind of co-ordinated, overt activity by hands, of speech etc. (FEU, Nov. 1982, p. 1, para. 3)

The FEU followed this up with an updated checklist (FEU, Nov. 1982, appendix 3), based on developed and extended aims, which importantly included reference to the skill of computer literacy. The aims cover skills in:

> language: (reading, writing, speaking and listening);
> number: (calculation, measurement, graphs and tables);
> manipulative dexterity and co-ordination;
> problem solving;
> everyday coping;
> interpersonal relationships;
> computer literacy, and learning
> – and experiences related to: –
> career options;
> work and society;
> economic and political problems;
> the environment; and
> values. (FEU, Nov. 1982, p. 2, para. 6)

The FEU's concept of skills has spread onto a much broader canvas, involving education as well as training. It is also apparent that the word 'basic' in 'basic skills' does not mean simple, or easy, or refer to low-level skills.

Presuming government's tacit acceptance of this broader perspective, the concept of the FEU ABC common core skills would remain fundamentally influential on this phase of the course. A difficulty in implementing the phase could be the prospect of mixed attainment/ability groupings of trainees. In these circumstances the phase could involve, for example, teachers in considerable remedial work with some individuals, while coping with trainees of significant recent attainment and ability. It is also the case that diagnostic assessment should continue during the phase to ascertain the aptitude and interests of the trainees, so that they may be guided toward the vocational (occupational) studies and experience of interest (relevance) to them, and suited to their aptitudes. Whether the FEU's concept of basic skills will permeate to practice at the level of YTS curriculum organizations themselves is, of course, increasingly doubtful.

The common core phase leads to the vocational studies phase through a curriculum process which enables trainees to sample (experience) skills and work associated with the IMS concept of occupational families. This is a grouping of occupations on the basis that they share common skills (see Figure 4). The principle behind the trainee's progression from common core skills training to vocational skills training is that those who show interest and aptitude in certain skills, say associated with clerical operations, would become involved with the occupational family in which those skills were most salient. An example of a practical implementation model for delivering a course conforming in general to the FEU Figure 4 concept is shown in Figure 5. The figure 4 model is held by the FEU as the 'ideal'. The Figure 5 model does not conform entirely to the 'ideal' because only one vocational area is shown. This suggests, or implies, that induction and vocational sampling is too narrowly based. The FEU reiterated its (June 1979, para. 18) (ABC) point:

> courses could not assume (if conforming to the 'ideal' model) even a provisional preference on the part of all students at enrolment, and that some kind of induction phase would be necessary to help them develop this.... There is therefore a need to design a college-wide and/or co-ordinated multi agency induction phase so that the vocational area in which the student chooses to progress is assisted by careers guidance and some real *sampling* experience of a number of vocational areas. (FEU, Nov. 1982, p. 105)

It is argued by the FEU, IMS (MSC) and government that these should be related to the local labour market. The overall complexity of

Figure 4.   Framework for Progression (over One or Two Years)

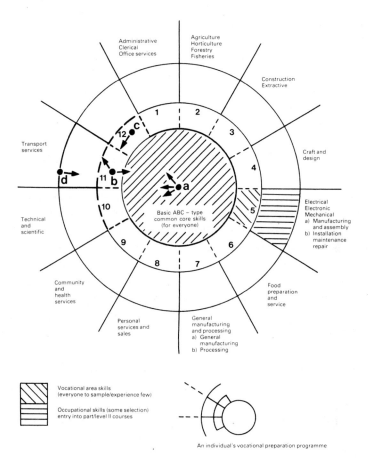

Source: FEU, Dec. 1981

this process is at once apparent. Trainees and tutors must 'somehow' negotiate and determine *individual* trainee's progression from common core skills to vocational training, in terms of local labour market prospects, the trainee's perception of his aptitude, attainment, interest, and the tutor's assessment of the same, and the capacity of the providing organization to actually deliver. The prospect of some very rough and ready practices developing to *cope* with this complexity is very high indeed. It is becoming increasingly clear that the ideal model of the FEU is negotiable. The construction industry, through the Training Board (CITB), has already been able to establish YTS proposals limited to the occupations of the industry. Many schemes eventually approved by Area Manpower Boards are sure to offer even more limited ranges of occupational experience.

However, it is assumed the trainee will *sensibly* progress from common core skills to sample those occupational skills included in a local training outline, and then locate with an occupational family and receive training and work experience in the skills associated with that family. It is during this period that careers advice and job vacancies information and guidance are likely to figure as an aspect of the 'new curriculum'. In other words, each trainee will begin the process of re-emerging onto the local labour market. Alternatively, trainees will begin the process of progressing from YTS to more 'advanced' relevant further training and/or education. This seems to mean 'relevant' in terms of a vocational course associated with the occupational family in which the trainee is receiving skills training and work experience.

In the present circumstances the trainee faces the prospect of moving from YTS, and its allowance of about £25 per week, to full-time education with no income whatsoever. Between this prospect and actually finding full-time employment is the possibility of finding a job which encompasses further training, either within a wholly company provided scheme, or with release to FE on a part-time basis. At this stage there is no obvious authoritative proposal to deal with trainees progressing to full-time FE, the official assumption being that trainees will find jobs in which progression through training is possible, or that they will simply remain unemployed. There is some room in the broad NTI proposals (Govt and MSC) for YTSs to be extended. It is to this possibility that FEU proposals might be directed. There are, as well, considerable institutional pressures for progression of this kind to become effectively possible by extension of the YTS from, in the first instance, one year to two. This would enable trainees to continue training and/or education at a more advanced level with allowances.

The problem of allowances is one of major proportions affecting all 16–19-year-olds not in jobs. Although addressed vigorously by interest groups in education, such as the National Association of Teachers in Further and Higher Education (NATFHE), the massive financial implications have made governments extremely wary of supporting any allowance scheme which implies extension to the whole 16–19 group. However, the Labour Party and the Alliance (SDP) have recently put forward proposals for a 16–19 education allowance or benefit. The problem was recognized by the Youth Task Group:

Figure 5. Blackpool and Fylde College of Further and Higher Education Implementation Model of Vocational Preparation in Construction

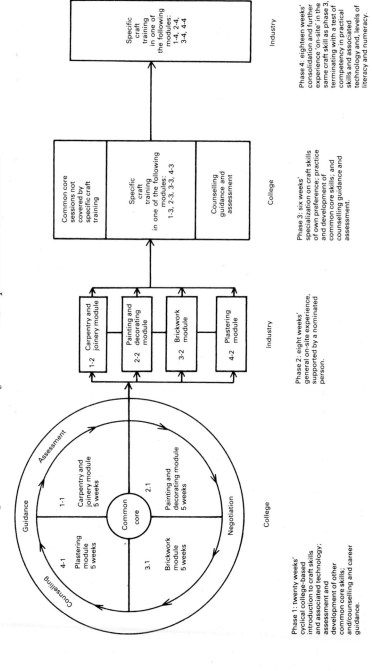

Source: based on FEU, Nov. 1982, p. 104.

This brings us to the wider question of financial support for young people age sixteen and seventeen. The scheme we recommend allows for employers to continue to recruit young people to jobs and pay them agreed wages. We believe that our scheme will be sufficiently attractive to employers and to young people for this group to be a relatively small minority. But the question is bound to arise of how the financial arrangements applying to those on our scheme relate to those for young people in full-time education. (MSC, *Youth Task Group Report*, April 1982, para. 7.12)

Entangled with this difficulty is the FEU concept of level 2, together with intimations of a relationship between YTSs and proposals for a new 17+ examination. Level 2 refers to the notion of accelerated entry for some YTS trainees to existing vocational FE courses. This requires validating bodies to recognize the 'new curriculum' as potentially 'qualificatory' in terms of entry to their courses (at level 2). The FEU described level 2 as:

At the moment 'Level-2' can only be described in terms of existing and educational/training programmes such as CGLI part II schemes, TEC Level II, BEC National, RSA II/III Certificates . . . and employers' second-year training schemes. Hopefully, however, implementation of the NTI objectives will encourage the recognition of many more 'Level-2' schemes based on experience and competence as well as on educational criteria, thus providing not only a wider spectrum of opportunity for young people, but more opportunities for adults. (FEU, Dec. 1981, para. 15)

It is, therefore, easy to appreciate that the interface between the 'new curriculum' and present FE curricula is, and is likely to remain, problematic. This despite the FEU's determination that basic skills importantly means '. . . those skills *basic* to a learner's progression into a higher education or training scheme' (FEU, Nov. 1982, p. 21, para. 61 (vi)). The ambiguity of the phrase 'higher education' in this context is noticeable. Trainees progressing through the 'new curriculum' are likely to move toward a complex, uncertain and ambiguous interface between what they do and what follows. The problem is manifold. The interface is between the 'new curriculum' and a possible range of 'progressions'. These are broadly: further or new unemployment; employment through local labour market characteristic demands;

unsupported further education and/or training; possible extension of their YTS for another year; employment with further education and/or training.

The FEU concept of progression for each individual trainee is subject to immense practical deficiencies in these circumstances. This could be especially the case in respect of trainees progressing either to a level 2 FE course, or continuing in a YTS for another year. Could the year 'count' as a level 2 year for FE validating bodies, or could trainees be accelerated and progress in their first YTS year by having it 'counted' as a level 2 entry qualification? Progression to further training may be supported in the context of the Youth Task Group Report recommendation for 'selective support' under a modified MSC 'Training for Skills Programme'. The implication is that some trainees could be selected as suitable for continuing support within a modified MSC scheme. It can be readily appreciated that both the level 2 concept and this 'selective support' possibility depend on the *selection* of some YTS trainees for continuation in more advanced curricula, either in FE, or the Skill Centre system, should it survive privatization.

The main consequence of the problems and difficulties associated with the interface between the 'new curriculum' and 'what follows', that is, the progression, is that the 'new curriculum' itself progresses or leads to confusion. As trainees proceed through the 'new curriculum' to choosing which family of occupational skills they will receive training and experience in, they actually progress toward a last phase which is by this time governed by the YTS's own *internal* logic. This is to say that the central impetus of the 'new curriculum' is toward employment, and through employment the further skills progression of the trainee. Continuing lack of employment prospects for some trainees, probably a substantial proportion, together with the present 'Hobson's choice' of progressing to no income and FE, or to an income through the dole, does nothing to ameliorate this confusion. The crisis between the internal logic of the 'new curriculum' and the external 'logic' of the interface will manifest itself during the last phase of the trainee's experience of the 'new curriculum', and will form part of that experience.

Involved with and compounding the problem of progression is the assessment process. There is a somewhat frenetic consensus that adequate standards should be applied to YTS courses and to the trainees in them. There is little doubt that a major feature of the 'new curriculum' should be the measurement and statement of the attainments of the trainees 'in a way which is recognisable, both to the young person, and to potential employers' (NTI, Dec. 1981, Govt, para. 26). One way of interpreting what is meant by attainment would be the measurement and statement of the progress of individual trainees, in other words a kind of (individualized) criterion-referenced assessment scheme, as opposed to a norm-referenced scheme. In spite of the drive for (national) standards it is possible to envisage an assessment process which is essentially formative leading to a summative conclusion which would show the *progress* of the individual trainee against the standard of his entry (profile) performance of common core (basic skills) criteria. However, it is clearly the case that a 'profile' of standards for the criteria relevant to work in general and, in particular, an occupation (job), may be used to measure trainees' exit performances. Included in such a 'profile' of standards would be measures of basic skills attainment.

If the FEU's 'changing concept' of basic skills is installed in the practice of YTSs, then it would generate the criteria for testing skills against a 'profile' of standards. Added to these would be occupational (job) criteria and their associated 'profile' of standards. The examination of trainees' performances against such an overall 'profile' of standards could lead to a complex passing/failing (achieving/not achieving) statement. The impression is that each of the standards for the performance of criteria is fixed (or to be fixed) and will form a kind of sacrosanct measure of the 'capacity' of a trainee to do something else, a job, another course.

In an important respect employers may see the YTS as a massive screening operation enabling them to select the most suitable of the trainees in individual company or industry-based YTSs for further employment and training; those not deemed suitable, that is, those who fail, will leave the employer with a YTS certificate of attainment. The MSC's Mode A additionality rules provide the financial basis upon which employers could be encouraged to use the YTS in this way. An MSC paper (MSC/82/N30) reporting on some of the employer-based pilot schemes carries indications that, even at this early stage of development, the schemes tend in the direction of a screening process for company recruitment. Related to this is the increasing certainty that employer-based YTSs may be structurally incapable of delivering multi-skills and transferable skill training. The tendency could be toward single skill courses. The MSC recognizes this difficulty, and has said this in respect of Occupational Training Families (OTFs):

> We [the MSC] have already made several references to broad based occupational training. At the same time, there is a limit to

what can be achieved in any one scheme. Managing Agents and Sponsors will not be expected to train everybody for everything. (MSC, Youth Training News, No. 1, Jan. 1983, p. 11)

The distinction is between single occupations and the jobs within an occupation. Such a distinction is easily blurred, if indeed it can be said to exist at all.

 The concepts of norm and criterion referencing are usually taken to be fairly distinct. However, it is by no means clear how criteria referents can be established without in practice incorporating norms for their performance. This is to say that the establishment of specific behaviours in domains as criteria by which performance is measured, must, in consequence, involve the determination of a behaviour, which is both measurable and *normally* achievable, as a result of (or in spite of) an instructional programme. In this sense, normal would mean a standard which it is *reasonable* or politic to set. This is a difficult but important distinction, because it illuminates a contradiction or confusion of purpose in the internal logic of examining the performance of YTS trainees. On the one hand, performance of identified basic skills and job related behaviours (criteria) must meet standards which are extrinsically established in the 'outside world' of industry (work). Consequently, they are only normally achievable to the extent that the population of the jobs in occupations is normal, that is, the present incumbents (population) can be said to be normal in relation to the normal population of YTS trainees. On the other hand, the 'new curriculum' should succeed in delivering young people from future structural unemployment. Success in this is seen to depend mainly on the concept of basic skills and less on job specific skills. The success of YTS courses, and the 'new curriculum' ensconced therein, will be to an extent measured in terms of the 'pass-rate' of trainees. Will those trainees who do not get jobs, but get a YTS certificate, have failed? Will it be necessary to ensure that the performance criteria of identified behaviours are measured against intrinsically established standards which reflect reasonably, that is, normally, achievable performance? Of course, the purpose of measuring trainees' performance is ostensibly to see if they can do certain things; and these may well be prescribed in behavioural terms against 'normal' criteria performance. Indeed, the emphasis of the 'new curriculum' aims on training for work, and the concomitant constriction of broader educational aims, suggests that such criterion referencing is appropriate. A list of 'trainees should be able to do ...', at stages in their programmes, could ensure that 'normal' trainees can do them. The problem of restricted range variation as it affects norm referencing, while not ceasing to affect criterion referencing, does cease to be problematic when not attempting to discern *differences* in ability/attainment.

> After reviewing the possible interpretations available, and their measurement and evaluation implications, it appears that the most defensible definition is the following: *A criterion-referenced test is used to ascertain an individual's status with respect to a well defined behaviour domain.* (Popham, 1975, p. 130)

Defining well behaviour domains related to basic and occupational skills must surely involve ascertaining what standards of performance trainees have to demonstrate in order to go on to do jobs or further training with reasonable prospects of succeeding. However, the 'half' likely to form the bulk of the YTS catchment is the bottom half. Will such criterion referencing lead in effect to mass failures (or low grade passes) with the inevitable suggestion that the scheme does not work? Or will the advent of a new skills pedagogy, trainee centre reviewing and negotiated profile certificates reveal a regenerated bottom half with newly released capacities for attainment which are presently restrained by the slavish bonds of inappropriate curricula and examinations? The immense financial and public political commitment to YTS is hardly likely to lead to a scheme which does not work. Who, at any level or kind of relation to the scheme, could countenance such a failure? Surely a normal YTS entrant should be able to pass. However, the assumption that YTS entrants are likely to form homogeneous low ability groups may not prove wholly accurate in the event. Unemployment is now so widespread among young people that YTS could catch-up a wide range of ability. However, it is a reasonable supposition that normality will form on the low ability range and that criterion referencing may need to ensure that the normal trainee can succeed. Concentration on psychomotor and basic cognitive skills will both occupy and improve trainees, while not inflaming their socio-economic perceptions, particularly when the work they do, as work experience or on-the-job training, will be paid at the training allowance level.

However, the quality of training and standards is thought to be important. There is persistent reference to quality training by the MSC. The Youth Task Group, no doubt with the needs of industry and politicians in mind, borrowed the term 'quality assurance' from the production line. Quality assurance was to be based on the formation of national criteria for course evaluation to be implemented by a National Supervisory Board (Inspectorate?).

> ... we recommend that the MSC should develop its capacity to ensure the quality of the scheme generally and, more specifically, to advise the Local Boards on the suitability of organizations applying to become Managing Agencies [YTS provider organizations]; to assist such agencies to establish and maintain standards; to evaluate the performance of such agencies; and generally to report on quality assurance matters. It should assign staff specifically to this work. (MSC, Youth Task Group Report, April 1982, para. 5.22, my parenthesis)

The initial stridence about standards has become somewhat muted in the light of the obvious practical difficulties of implementing any kind of centralized inspectorate to govern standards over such an extensive and diverse conglomerate as the YTS. An MSC Advisory Group on Contents and Standards has been formed to '... set minimum criteria for the framework around which managing agents and sponsors will design their own programmes' (MSC, Youth Training News, No. 1, Jan. 1983, p.7). Area Manpower Boards will have the final say whether a programme can go forward or not. They will have discretion to approve programmes which do not meet minimum national criteria. The practice of the 'new curriculum', therefore, could be subjected to general guidance and scrutiny by a form of national inspectorate, filtered and diluted by Area Manpower Boards. This has considerable significance for the process of assessing individual trainees, by way of the relationship between the 'success' and satisfaction of individual trainees, and a measurement of the efficacy or 'quality' of particular whole courses. The interrelatedness of standards for evaluating YTS courses and standards for evaluating individual trainees is usefully explored by the IMS (Feb. 1982, paras 2.3 ff), along with some other issues to do with standards.

The IMS recognized the extensiveness and laboriousness of attempting definitions of standards for learning objectives (para. 2.3.9). It also recognized the nature of the prolonged debate about the role and function of examinations and practical testing. However, if, as the Youth Task Group suggested, Managing Agencies are to be accredited in some degree by means of 'inspection', then the points made by the IMS on accreditation of sponsors become central. The IMS pointed out that standards in relation to the authorization or approval of sponsors may cover one or more aspects of traineeships.

In simple systems terms, standards may be laid down about *inputs* to the traineeship, about *process* during the traineeship or about *outputs* of the traineeship. Translated into standards relating to sponsors, this means that sponsors may be asked to meet criteria regarding:

- administrative and organisational arrangements (inputs);
- syllabuses and learning objective (process);
- levels and types of achievement by trainees at the end of traineeships (outputs). (IMS, Feb. 1982, para. 2.3.10)

This is close to the CIPP approach of Stufflebeam (1974) – Context, Inputs, Process, Product. The CIPP definition of evaluation involves centrally the provision of information. Popham (1975, p. 36) reports:

Stufflebeam has attempted to relate the CIPP model to Scriven's (1967) formative and summative evaluation. In reconciling these constructs, Stufflebeam distinguishes between *evaluation for decision making* and evaluation for accountability. He believes that when evaluation serves a formative role it is *proactive* and is aimed at abetting decision-makers. When, however, evaluation serves a summative role it is *retroactive* in nature and is aimed to serve as a basis for accountability.

The IMS went on to speculate on possible combinations of the three aspects (Inputs, Process, Outputs) which could be used as bases for establishing standards for courses. However, with the Youth Task Group Report in mind, and the stress the government and MSC have placed on the provision of a 'recognizable' record of standards achieved by the individual trainee, it is very likely that *outputs* standards will receive significant scrutiny as a measure of the standard (quality) of YTS courses.

The implication is, then, that the 'inspectorial' evaluation of YTS courses will be in the summative mode and be retroactive in nature, being in effect designed to serve as a basis for accountability. If output (product) scrutiny forms a highly significant aspect of such evaluation, then such scrutiny will surely act reflexively upon the 'new curriculum'. Accepting this as exceedingly likely, then the 'new curriculum' would include a major element of experience to do with testing for the trainees, in both a material and psychological pass/fail framework. The form of individual certification is not yet (March 1983) established.

However, Managing Agencies will be *given* a format for the certificate soon. Presumably, this will take on the guise of a national MSC certificate, and will be expressed in the form of a profile document showing '. . . what occupational skills knowledge and experience the trainees have gained; what the trainees can do in the five core areas, and any other activities . . .' (MSC, Youth Training News, No. 1, Jan. 1983, p. 10). Trainees' achievements should be indicated against standards 'where appropriate', or, perhaps, where they have been worked out. Profiling based on trainee-centred reviewing is certainly indicated as an aspect of providing certification. This remains in keeping with the Youth Task Group's thinking,

> In order to convince young people and others of the value of the scheme, there must be provision for recognized certification of achievement by young people within the scheme and this must facilitate the progression of young people to further training, immediately or later in life; (MSC, *Youth Task Group Report,* April 1982, para. 3.15 H)

In the earlier MSC document (*NTI*, Dec. 1981, MSC) agreement seemed clear that 'standards need to be based firmly on the skills, knowledge and experience actually required in the performance of a job or range of jobs' (para. 2). It went on to say:

> This implies a system in which there is much greater flexibility in the way training is done but greater uniformity in the levels of competence of those completing training. The system must show what an individual can do and not where he has failed. So standards will need to be:
> (i) EXPLICIT: so that firms and individuals know what they are and where information about them can be obtained;
> (ii) AGREED: so that there can be no doubt about them and their standing;
> (iii) WIDELY ACCESSIBLE: to young people and to adults;
> (iv) FLEXIBLE: in response to the changing, and sometimes different, needs of individuals and localities through a variety of forms of provision (eg education, full-time and part-time training);
> (v) PROGRESSIVE: so that people with a 'portfolio' of skills, knowledge and experience can build on that as they

> seek to adapt to technological and market changes, to improve their prospects or to explore their potential;
>
> (vi)   TESTABLE: so that they embody an agreed, appropriate and common standard of training achievement which can be certified as such. (*NTI*, Dec. 1981, MSC, para. 21)

It could be surmised, therefore, that it is by no means clear whether 'certification' of trainees at the end of their courses will in effect be norm-referenced or criterion-referenced. The committee (and one is reminded of camels) of the MSC seems to want both a common standard and a means of showing what the individual trainee can do. Clarity is required, but also a measurement of the *individual* trainee's achievement, perhaps the grade of the trainee in comparison to the population of trainees. This would explain why there is no reference to measuring the input attainment of trainees to enable individual *progress* to be measured. It seems, then, that trainee leaving profiles, as summative assessments, are to be 'criterion-referenced' against common standards or norms; in other words, the criteria used for referencing are to be identified, and common measures established, in relation to basic and occupational skills requirements, as a means of founding common standards. Consequently, individual progression on a course could range from virtually nil to the very substantial, while yet meeting the common standards, by which both the quality of the trainee and, to a significant extent, the quality of the course is to be measured. If this is the case, the leaving profiles will, in effect, record the testing of trainees against norms in the way of normal examinations, although not in the form of normal examinations. Therefore, it is inevitable that some trainees will 'pass' and others will 'fail'; and that some will get good passes and others poor, and so on. It is important to recognize this effect because of its significance as part of the curriculum. Without rehearsing the well known and extensively published arguments about the practical effects on curriculum implementation of the pass/fail examination syndrome, it is sufficient to say that, whatever form the profiling takes, it will inevitably affect the 'new curriculum' as examination, although of complex and extensive assembly and certification format. Certificates may, as already suggested, be treated as a form of comparative grading.

An Institute of Personnel Management survey covering organizations in all employment sectors and some three million workers concluded that:

A profile, or any other selection tool, would not be used in isolation. It appears that a profile would be valuable in contributing to selection decisions in the following ways:

– distinguishing between candidates . . . .   80 per cent
– assessing suitability for training course. . . . .   72 per cent
– assessing suitability for particular job
  vacancy. . . . .   83 per cent
– analysing candidates' strengths and
  weaknesses . . . .   78 per cent
– determining a particular training
  programme . . . .   70 per cent

(FEU, Sept. 1982 (Wood, S.), p. 80, para. 7.81)

The sample profile used in the survey was designed by the FEU. It can be seen from the above result that profiles will be used to distinguish materially between candidates and to assess their suitability for jobs or for training. Although not overtly graded, profile certificates are labels attached to individuals which could substantially determine whether they succeed in the job market or not.

The FEU's draft student profile, used in the IPM survey, is regarded by the Scottish Vocational Preparation Unit (SVPU) as a type of report which '. . . offers a much greater number of judgements over a wider focus of cognitive and affective behaviours – the student is made more visible' (Scottish Vocational Preparation Unit, 1982, p. 7). The SVPU points out that the difference between reports and records is important, and that the following distinction is often fudged: 'A *record* is evidence on which outsiders can make judgements. A *report* is judgement which outsiders can take as evidence. A record is therefore open; a report closed' (*ibid.*). A conclusion drawn by the SVPU is that most current profiles are extensions of norm-referenced labelling as used in public examinations. Such profiles are actually expanded reports and not records. What they do is provide much more detailed failure labels than other examinations.

However, the SVPU's extensive recommendations are largely based on producing profiles which are trainee-negotiated, trainee-centred, trainee-led, open in form, trainee-formative and that the curriculum is, in effect, assessment-led, and, as assessment is trainee-centred and negotiated, curriculum is trainee-led. Apart from being radical, the SVPU's recommendations are so resource intensive that they might seem utopian to the MSC and government. The idea of so much trainee involvement in the certification process might seem more like self-certification to employers. Problematic words like 'collusion' could attach themselves to the process. However, teachers may be attracted to the possibility of this approach being a way of 'selling' students their own profiles. Getting students to recognize their own shortcomings may be a good idea, and, in any case, finally induce them to collude in the certification of their own failures. However, the SVPU has at least refused to compromise on the issue of the purpose and function of profiling, namely, to operate formatively in the service of the individual trainee. The resulting profile records should belong to the trainee, and 'institutions should not provide information from such records – in any form – without the permission of the trainee' (*ibid.*, p. 62, para. 6).

The FEU, by arguing that YTS courses should provide for planned progression to FE vocational training and education, tacitly accepts that norm-referenced examination is inevitable, while arguing that '. . . a significant amount of selection is beginning to take place on MSC YOP schemes and that too could become divisive' (FEU, *Progressing from Vocational Preparation,* Dec. 1981, para. 12). However, in the previous paragraph of the same paper it argued:

> It is already possible to find young people who have, since the age of fifteen, experienced a variety of pre-vocational courses including work experience, but in terms of conventional educational and training schemes, they remain unacceptable and apparently inferior to their peers with more conventional examination successes. In short, we are in danger of perpetuating a form of intellectual apartheid if we allow, by neglect or design, vocational preparation to become a non-progressive mode of educational/training provision, having all the characteristics of a 'tertiary modern' sector and by implication associated with low ability school leavers. (*ibid.*, para. 11)

However, any impression that YTS profiles will in practice record students' progress without in effect providing an extensive and detailed differentiation between their achievements, and by implication their abilities, is obviously nonsense. Consequently, YTS students will be examined, continuously and (if justly and accurately) complicatedly over the whole period of their courses. The results of this criterion-structured examination, however much negotiated between examiner/tutor and student, will state categorically what the student cannot do. The shape and extent of the scale of standards will indicate this clearly (ticks = passes, blanks = fails). The average profile (surely this will emerge) will provide the norm reference in a very short time. In addition, the ticking process in filling out a profile is flagrantly subjective. What on earth does the tick mean here?

> – has developed background knowledge necessary for general
>   understanding of national and local government.   □
>   (FEU, Draft Student Profile Record, Sept. 1982)

Of course, the problem of subjectivity is not a simple one. Involved is the almost awesome difficulty of communalizing the meanings of the descriptors, the actual language used to describe the criteria to be tested, and the language used to describe the related standards. Add to this the difficulties of making these explicit, not only to the thousands of unqualified and half qualified examiner/tutors, but to employers, the public and indeed to the students. Add to this the need for commonality not only of criteria, language and standards, but in the curriculum itself across a wide range of Managing Agencies requiring *flexibility*, and the ideals of profiling in respect of the YTS 'new curriculum' seem very far-fetched. This is not even to consider the *immense* resource implications of a profiling system for YTSs which will be fundamentally formative in process for the student *and* curriculum led, *and* effectively summative in certification. Consequently, the practice of profiling is likely to be less than ideal, resulting in the widespread 'ticking' of an MSC delivered profile format, supplemented by earnest in-service training seminars. The conclusion that the bottom half is yet again to be the subject of under-resourced experiment is hard to avoid. Employers were already indicating (March 1983) that they were incapable of administering a profiling system of anything approaching FEU and educationist aspirations. Although the MSC seems publicly firm on its major previous commitments to standards, there is tacit acceptance that employer-based schemes will simply certify in some way or other (ticks or crosses?) that the trainee has met the standards (?) of his MSC YTS course. This piece of paper may create yet another false consensus between those who cannot be bothered to develop and administer a difficult system and those who disapprove, in any case, of the potential totalitarian nature of detailed and sophisticated public records of the judgements made by teachers and supervisors about trainees, especially those judgements in the affective domain.

Certainly the FEU sees the YTS as an opportunity to get under way its broad strategic aim of vocational preparation for all, although immediately related to a new 17+ examination and some undefined prospect of progression for that 'bottom half' of leavers presently neglected by the education system. It presumes that intellectual apartheid will be reduced eventually, and that, in the meantime, low ability school leavers will learn core skills and 'pass' the new profiling examinations in substantial numbers, and thus have their abilities recognized. Such recognition would be of their performance of core (basic) skills, and of their general capacities, which are not tested or described by failure or success in the cognitive/content testing of conventional examinations (particularly GCE). Nevertheless,

> (iii) for certification to be acceptable, competence related to many of the performance-related objectives of the common-core will have to be measured. The corollary of this is the possibility that some students may not attain these levels of competence before the end of the course. (FEU, June 1979, para. 81 (iii))

It is clear, then, that the FEU bases its position on the assumption that low ability leavers are largely (normally) able to achieve competence in common core skills, and that it is not at present open to them to have this recognized through the conventional examination system. However, it recognizes, too, that some will fail the 'new' system. The inference to be drawn, presumably, is that 'new curriculum' trainees should be examined in terms of the FEU's suggestions in *A Basis for Choice* (June 1979), drawing on its later collage of views in *Profiles* (Sept. 1982).

The foregoing suggests that the FEU approach is not in any simple sense incompatible with MSC and government objectives. However, it is doubtful if the substantive political objectives of the Conservative government and the ostensibly educational objectives of the FEU are compatible. Essentially, the FEU is trying to install vocational preparation into the education system as a Trojan Horse hauled by the machinery and resources of the MSC. Such installation is congruent with much apparently radical individual and institutional opinion in education, and would depend upon a change of government for its real fruition. It is possible, however, that, once installed, vocational preparation will in any case, spill out into the system, becoming a modifying force of significant effect, which could in time bring about a major new curricular facility for *all* pupils and not just bottom half minimum age leavers. The government's New Training and Vocational Education Initiative may, however, eventually succeed in establishing vocational preparation in the secondary system as an alternative curriculum to run alongside an improved grammar curriculum for top leavers leading to

A-levels and professional or higher education qualifications. The government's main objective in the short term is to reduce youth unemployment figures with the YTS, and to use it as well as a means of restructuring the system of training for skills in the labour market. The idea is to make all skills training, including apprenticeships, more efficient and effective and to eradicate time-serving. The MSC's objective is to put into effect one means or instrument for implementing a national manpower policy, which they have a responsibility to formulate, and do, under the Employment and Training Act 1973. Training is, of course, a major instrument in the MSC's overall manpower strategy, first clearly expressed in its major document, *Towards a Comprehensive Manpower Policy* (October 1976).

In this last respect it is important to emphasize that the YTS is only a component of a broader manpower policy, and is, even in this, subsumed under the New Training Initiative's general objectives (see Chapter 2). The Construction Industry Training Board (CITB), for example, is sensitive to this point:

> The publication of the YTS which the MSC has developed to achieve Objective 2 (of the three objectives for the NTI), has tended to create the impression that the YTS and NTI are synonymous. This is not correct. The objectives are clearly inter-related and the MSC places greater emphasis on the achievement of the objectives as a whole than only on YTS. (CITB, 1982, para. 18)

The CITB (October 1982) paper went on to point up the underlying aim of the NTI as providing access for a person, irrespective of route of entry and age, to skilled work through the achievement of recognized standards. The CITB, along with other industrial training interests, is concerned about the time-serving element in apprentice-type training, which is seen as a central obstruction to the flexible and sufficient supply of skilled manpower to industry. Underlying the traditional process of training through the apprentice system is the historic perspective of craft unions, namely their need to control the labour market, or at least influence supply of skilled labour. The printing unions are supposedly the bastions of such a perspective. However, agreement was reached on major changes in training and recruitment between the British Printing Industries Federation (BPIF) and the National Graphical Association (NGA) in January 1983. Members of the NGA voted four to one in favour of the changes on the recommendation of their National Council. The agreement is very much in line with the NTI objectives as a whole:

> Essential features of the new Agreement are flexible entry to NGA occupations, including provision for the recruitment of adults as well as school leavers; variable training periods determined by the time needed in individual circumstances to achieve agreed standards (rather than on a fixed period of 'time-serving'); a log book system; and relevant printing education studies. (British Printing Industries Federation, Circular, 28 January 1983)

In summary, YTS courses are obviously only an aspect of wider training developments for employment, in the somewhat complex and general context of a national manpower policy based on uncertain projections and political futures. However, so far as YTS courses are concerned, trainees are likely to belong to 'new curriculum' organizations in which they experience a major process of checking or testing leading to their leaving with 'results' in the shape of profiles formed along the lines already adumbrated by the FEU, and given national shape by an MSC issued form. The profiles would be certificates of the competence of trainees in common core skills and related occupational family skills, together with delineations of their general character, capacities and progress. It is clear that the Youth Task Group's recommendation for a form of 'inspectorate' of standards and the setting of national standards implied that common core skills are fertile ground for the testing, providing a basis for profile statements of common national validity (and hence acceptability) between Managing Agencies. Commonality of standards would come from common measures for profiling, at least the common core skills.

The FEU, in 1979, recognized profiling as appropriate to certification (recording judgements): 'We think that a profile system is the most appropriate means of recording assessment of both common core and the vocational and job specific studies' (FEU, June 1979, para. 90). The profile should be simple and '... record the results of any formal or objective tests of appropriate attainment, as well as evidence derived from course work and from the subjective evaluation of other relevant abilities. It will also serve as a general indication of the activities undertaken by students during the course' (*ibid.*, para. 95 F).

The example given then by the FEU of profiling in practice drew on the work of the Scottish Council for Research in Education, which reported on, and outlined, the use of profiles for skills, subjects/

activities and other observations. The YTS 'new curriculum' and its YOP predecessor have attracted considerable profile development work since then. The YTS is thought to offer great scope and at long last a substantial home for profiling advocates. However, it is doubtful if YTS profiling will, in the short term, materialize as a radical practice, but may, perhaps, serve as a precursor for the sort of broad educational change envisaged by Adams and Burgess (1980) and others. Certainly this seems to be the view of Jack Mansell, the FEU Director:

> Ultimately, however, the argument for profiles is an educational one in the broadest sense. That is to say it is about helping individuals to develop by recording in a supportive way the knowledge, skills and experience they individually possess.
> (FEU, September 1982, p. 9, para. 2.2.6)

In the immediate term YTS trainee profile 'certificates' could provide a means of determining whether the trainee has reached or could reach level 2, and in this way indicates a suitable course of vocational progression for that trainee in further education; it would be a 'pass' in this respect. It should also provide employers with sufficient information about, and indicators of, the trainee's performance on the course and capabilities for future work; it will be to that extent a summative, criterion-referenced pass or fail indicator, together with an information base about the personality or affective attributes of trainees to inform the judgements of potential employers. In this last respect the 1979 A–Z study of the Industrial Training Research Unit reported a list of attributes that employers valued in young people. The list is interesting for its quite clear indication that employers would like to know if young people have, or have the potential for, versatility; initiative; taking pride in the job; forming good personal relations; listening (well) to instructions; having a wide viewpoint; seeking more work if slack; being quality conscious; being good timekeepers; asking questions; being methodical and neat; reporting faults; remedying problems. To provide such information about individual trainees is to enter the problematic area of assessment in the affective domain. The difficulties of this kind of assessment activity have been succinctly expressed by Black and Dockrell (1980). They posed the question, 'assessment in the affective domain: do we, can we, should we?' They concluded that in practice teachers do make such assessments, on a commonsense basis, but not publicly,

> . . . it is clear that the affective component is little used in the process of formal certification, although in some cases, eg the

> Schools Council Integrated Science 'O' level and many CSE
> examinations, a small proportion of the total mark may be
> obtained from teachers' affective assessments. Yet, at the time,
> teachers manifestly do make judgements about the affective
> characteristics of their students, not least in the supply of
> testimonials, references and UCCA forms. (Black and Dock-
> rell, 1980, p. 199)

Obviously, much is said in testimonials, references and UCCA
forms by omission, or faint praise (blanks). The testimonial is particularly vulnerable to devaluation, because of its public nature. However,
Black and Dockrell concluded that affective intentions in education are
widely acceptable to teachers, but teachers were equally divided over
the question of including such material on national certificates as an
endorsement made at the level of the school. It is one thing to give
personal, if detached, opinion about pupils in the affective domain, and
another to formulate and certify a detached assessment of national
currency and public expression. Nevertheless, the work of Black and
Dockrell suggests that teachers do make assessments in the affective
domain based on commonsense, technically known as simple implicit
personality theory. However, creating a common or shared set of
descriptors and measures for assessment in the affective domain
requires considerable research and development, and, in the event of
the formation of such instruments, considerable effort to install a
national system. Employers clearly make judgements about the suitability of young people for employment which include at present
commonsense measures related to the descriptors identified by the
A–Z study (IRTU, 1979). YTS profiles would, however, be public,
and assessments in the affective domain expressed through them, while
desirable, could easily reduce to testimonials only marginally related to
the notion of national and recognizable standards. As the emerging
aims of the 'new curriculum' substantially include teaching and assessment in the affective, the question whether teachers *should* assess and
publicly report their judgements becomes an increasingly significant
moral as well as a technical one.

Apart from serving as a certificate, profiles could be used as
curriculum evaluation data. The success of the 'new curriculum' could
be importantly evaluated on the output model accountability basis.
Obviously this would not evaluate the 'new curriculum' properly, but
it is likely to appeal because of its administrative convenience and, in
any case, be perceived by teachers and Managing Agents as an

important measure of their success in running YTS courses. This would be particularly so in resolving the tension between criterion referencing against nationally recognized standards and the assumption that the norm of the bottom half will pass or meet such standards. It follows that profiling is likely to be a major area of tension for trainees, between trainees and teachers, between teachers and the managers of YTS courses, and between the managers and the Managing Agencies as bodies in relation to Area Manpower Boards. Add to this the considerable feature of schooling in the affective domain at the heart of the YTS 'new curriculum', and the profiling process is arguably totalitarian in character.

A key feature, then, of the 'new curriculum' is the process of performance assessment and collation of information about the trainee throughout the course. Teachers are to be placed in an ambiguous authority relationship to the trainees. This is because they are in effect, to pass or fail them, while at the same time teach them, and importantly, as well, to counsel and guide them. Meetings between trainees and teachers for counselling and guidance purpose will be inescapably bound up with the teacher's view of individual trainees. Notes and records of counselling and guidance meetings will necessarily become involved with the profiling process. The advantages to the teaching process of the teacher/pupil conspiracy, or solidarity, to defeat the 'examiners' are inevitably lost. This alliance between teacher and pupil to overcome and succeed together against an external examination system is one of far deeper significance than is often recognized.

The 'new curriculum' places teachers in the difficult position of being themselves the 'externals', while requiring them to develop and secure the role of mentor, advisor, counsellor in the perception of trainees. The fact that the 'success' of their trainees could also be a significant measure of their own success, and the success of the providing organization, is likely to be a stressful compound of pressures to dilute standards, and connive against the 'inspectorate'. It is not sufficient to argue that CSE Mode 3 assessment or current practice in public sector further and higher education is similar to the emergent YTS assessment method and, therefore, not new. They may marginally resemble it in different ways, but there are substantial differences. There is a definite role for external validation and moderation in public sector further and higher education practices, much related to the setting and marking of written work. In the case of CSE Mode 3, there is often an almost complete lack of external credibility for the certificates. Whether this perception is fair or not to the efforts of individual institutions and teachers cannot be simply determined. The various factors of credibility, kind of material coverage of assessment, the authority and role of validators and moderators and teachers are complexly interrelated. The 'Catch 22' in profiling is that the simpler and shallower the depth of the format of the final summative certificate, the more obviously it will approach the traditional graded pass-fail certificate, or reduce to mere testimonial of little credibility. Alternatively, the more extensive its coverage of performance criteria and the deeper the control over standards, then the more totalitarian it becomes, especially in terms of its reflexive effects upon YTS curriculum organizations. It is naive to suppose that extensive testing in depth, leading to detailed summative certification, would not substantially influence the experience of trainees as members of such a curriculum organization. The argument that all this would be curriculum-led, and not vice versa, is also naive. Such views spring from the remoter quarters of FE management, somewhat disconnected from the realities of the chalk-face and a basic knowledge of organization theory and practice. Over and above all this is the potential invidiousness of preparing *public* profiles on individual trainees, profiles which are effectively pass or fail certificates plus explanatory or justificatory material. They are in this respect dramatically different to school reports about a pupil's progress and prospects of passing an external examination, and, of course, entirely different in character to the confidential reference.

Without discussing at this stage the extensive socio-political-educationalist arguments in support of profiling, it is nevertheless clear that the problem of teachers as personal examiners, and the reflexion of this new relationship between pupil and teacher into the curriculum process itself, has barely been addressed. Broadfoot (1980, p. 70), in reviewing the Scottish Pupil Profile System, concludes:

> It is to be hoped that the development work of the Pupil Profiles Project, which has found favour around the world, will be extended at the earliest opportunity to an examination of the potential of the 'Negotiated' record. Only then will we even begin to approach a genuinely comprehensive sixteen-plus certification.

It is, perhaps, through the introduction of negotiation between teachers and trainees that a compromise can be reached between the conflict of roles the teacher will find himself in as a passer or failer of trainees. *Trainee Centred Reviewing* (MSC, Nov. 1981) reflects the experience gained in the perspective of formative profiling on different MSC youth schemes, including YOP. Its pedagogic benefits seem agreed, however employers' doubts about the summative process could not be disguised. There is certainly an intrinsic contradiction between formative trainee centred reviewing as a pedagogic process and its culminative use as summative certification. In any case, as already discussed, it is by no means clear that 'standards', as comprehended by employers, government, or indeed the MSC, can be maintained in terms of 'acceptability' or 'recognition', if the certification (profile) is negotiated with the student. What is clear is that the 'new curriculum' is likely to be bedevilled by teachers' role conflict, and/or the pressure of inspectoral/evaluative and other external expectations, together with trainee perceptions and motivations in respect of these.

Notwithstanding these likely difficulties is the addition of an extensive and intensive profiling administrative activity being inextricably bound up in the curriculum process. Added to which, and associated with it, is the inevitable complexity, even intricacy, of the organization and management of YTS courses overall. In particular, the organization, management and administration of the profiling process will have to span the entire course, and accommodate considerable individual detail about each trainee in the form of an information file of sufficient scope to enable an accurate and just and subsequently justifiable (or provable) public profile.

Winter (1976) describes some of the serious difficulties in producing 'files' to assist in the school process as a whole, and indicates, too, the problems of validity and alienation when such files go public to employers. In this context his section on 'Bureaucratic information: Sociological perspectives' (pp. 83–5) has considerable relevance to this aspect of the 'new curriculum'. Some of the key points are sketched below.

Winter, drawing on Weber, points out that authority in bureaucratic organizations is rigidly hierarchical and importantly dependent for rational decision-making on the use of files. However, files tend to be used to *justify* management decisions. Bureaucratic files can be considered as ways of legitimizing the exercise of power. He goes on to demonstrate that superiors have access to files on inferiors, but not vice versa; and that the distribution of knowledge is a clue to the distribution of power (cf. Handy, 1976). Files reflect not only the perspective of the individual member (raiser) of the institutional staff, but in some way the purposes of the institution itself. The file is a potential justification for an anticipated range of future actions (to give a good reference, to promote/demote to a different set, to pass, to fail, to warn parents, to recommend a particular curriculum/course, etc.)

The contents of a trainee's (pupil's) file can thus be seen as a build-up to the justification of an estimate of his market value. The school, Winter continues, contracts with the employer and the pupil to 'get it right', but in terms of the institutional purpose of the files. As the scale of operations become larger, institutional decision-making comes to depend more and more on information which is further and further away from the experience to which it relates, and which is pre-packaged in the light of administrative purposes. Files make possible the removal of decisions from the social contexts in which their origins and results are experienced. He concludes:

> In a capitalist economic system alienating relationships of production transform the industrial worker and his product into commodities for the commercial market; in a capitalist education system alienating relationships of perception and communication [for example amongst other things, the creation by staff of files on pupils] transform the pupil and his school work into commodities for the employment market. (Winter, 1976, p. 85)

Returning to Figure 3 in Chapter 3, it can be seen that periodic recording of counselling/guidance interviews will be necessary, together with precise recording of periodic assessments and tests. It is at once obvious that there is potential for teacher debilitation to be high. In other words, the administrative 'overhead', in terms of teacher energy, is likely to be very high indeed. Add to this the pressures already mentioned, and the likelihood is that either the 'chalk-face' will be weak and supported by piles of paper, or the paperwork will be thin and the 'chalk-face' undemonstrably strong, or, through general confusion, neither will stand much scrutiny.

Apart from such speculation, it remains the case that membership of a 'new curriculum' organization could well impart a significant experience to the trainee of being monitored, tested and recorded to pass/fail ends. Trainee perception of the role of teachers cannot be entirely separated from course work initiated by them. In other words, trainees' perception of the curriculum organization will involve their perception of the role of the teachers. Indeed, the perceived role of the teachers is surely part and parcel of trainees' perception of the 'new curriculum' when treating curriculum as an organization. There may be some effect of increasing the 'authority' of teachers, because of their direct influence over the profiles. However, as authority figures, teachers may end up with alienated trainees; alienated in terms of the counselling relationship which figures large in the 'new curriculum' as a crucial formative and pedagogic process. This point is developed in Chapter 4.

Nevertheless, and in spite of these intimations of difficulty, the 'new curriculum' is likely to provide a major opportunity for large numbers of leavers to obtain something to show for efforts they may make as members of their organization which is of sufficient detail to mitigate the present, almost total, lack of paper qualification open to those who do not sit, or fail, CSE or GCE examinations. The danger, of course, is that the YTS certificate could prove to be a negative qualification, that is, a certificate identifying and highlighting failure of the normal system of examination. However, the profile approach, by providing significant positive detail of a trainee's performance, may reduce this effect, an effect which resides, of course, in the present fixation of employers and the public in general with the GCE as the only 'real' qualification, a fixation recognized and accepted by pupils and parents alike, much to the chagrin of reformers.

In practical terms the 'new curriculum' is being taken up and advanced within FE in terms of LEAs being Managing Agencies for YTSs or suppliers of subsidized off-the-job minimum thirteen weeks training. A study of schemes being installed by the Bedfordshire LEA, the Sheffield Metropolitan District Council (Sheffield Five Colleges) and Avon LEA shows at once a major recognition of the need for the improved scheme to largely replace their present operations for MSC special programmes (mainly UVP, YOP, and WEEP). The Bedfordshire and Sheffield proposals are very fully described in NATFHE, Education Department Circular 29/82 of 29 March 1982. The Avon Scheme is described and analyzed in Edwards (1982), drawing on local correspondence, LEA minutes and circulars. Even a cursory analysis of these reveals the influence of the FEU. All three schemes conform to the pattern illustrated by Figure 3. There is considerable emphasis on transferability of skills, of their generic character (common core), on progression to work and/or further training, vocational preparation, or further vocational education, and on counselling, guidance and assessment, culminating in 'effective' leaving profiles for each trainee. There is a common emphasis, too, on the individual personal development of the trainee, with life and personal skills receiving clear specification as an element in the curriculum. Management and consultative structures in each of the examples are ramified, usually comprising five or six levels, each being composed of every possible interested party. In all cases the lowest level is the chalk-face comprised of teachers, organizers and administrators and, at some point it is to be supposed, the trainees. The management and consultative structures are aimed at accommodating the various, indeed, multifarious range of formal and informal influence groups, from councillors to MSC to industry to unions to LEA officers to voluntary bodies to college representatives to Careers Service to curriculum developers and *more* – indeed, a veritable pot-pourri of simmering designs upon the MSC's pot of gold. Beyond these immediate layers of interest are inchoate area and national mechanisms of inspection and accounting governed by the MSC.

Beneath this enormous (dead?) weight of interested negotiation lies the 'new curriculum', struggling for the breath of life, in the form of clear direction, trainees and sufficient resources to ensure the feasibility of implementing its sophisticated and 'revolutionary' aims. Early on, the Association of Colleges in Further and Higher Education concluded that the old funding rates system to colleges by the MSC gave a viable financial base for the courses (YOP, UVP), but that the new scheme provided a basis 'quite insufficient to meet college costs' (ACFHE, 1982, para. 5.2). The politics of funding was seriously engaged in determining whether LEAs would 'subsidize' the MSC's contribution to YTS. The arguments are predictable and will not be rehearsed here. However, from the beginning the 'new curriculum' faced major uncertainty on the resources front at the 'chalk-face', in spite of the managerial/political arena being crowded with protagonists, proposals, publicity and paper, not to mention political imperatives.

> Avon County Council is pressing for changes in the present government proposals. But for 1982–83, with financial backing of £2½ million from the Manpower Services Commission, a pilot scheme in Avon, offering 700 new youth training places, is assured.

> But the County Council has said that if future funding of YTS, as now proposed by the government, is not changed then it will have to pull out of the scheme after twelve months – a move that would only be taken with the deepest regret. (Avon Report, No. 9, August 1982; Avon County Council is Labour controlled).

Early in 1983 agreement was reached between the MSC Youth Training Board and the Confederation of British Industry (CBI), the Association of County Councils (ACC), the Association of Metropolitan Authorities (AMA), on a national funding rate for YTS further education in colleges (£14.70 per hour). This represents a one-third discount on what would otherwise be the full cost. To what extent some individual LEAs will be satisfied with the settlement is not clear. One important political effect of the agreement is the recognition (or capitulation of LEAs) that YTS will be partly funded by the education service, although control will still remain firmly at the centre with the MSC. LEAs' influence through funding will be restricted to that aspect of the 'new curriculum' delivered by the education service for industrial and other Managing Agencies. As payment for that service is to be subsidized by the Authorities, then the potential for under-resourcing is unquestionably high. Even if Authorities act themselves as Managing Agencies, they will remain caught in the same position, in effect subsidizing themselves from the MSC trainee block grant (£1850). It is very noticeable indeed that the aspect of 'education' in the YTS 'new curriculum' is the subject of tight financing in the particular.

In spite of all the uncertainties and difficulties surrounding the 'new curriculum', it seems that the English education system will shortly be engaged in a potentially revolutionary development in the making. Its most obvious feature is the partial, but wide, raising of the school leaving age, in conjunction with the personal financing of the leavers who become YTS trainees, with all the implications this has for all 16–19-year-olds in full-time education. The 'new curriculum' could suffer a crisis of internal logic in terms of a confusion about progression to further vocational training and education for trainees moving from a course with personal allowances to other courses presently without such provision. However, there is at present political scope for selective support in this respect becoming available, and perhaps more coherent and universal provision should there be a change of government. The 'new curriculum', too, has in effect largely subsumed itself under the curricular principles of pre-vocational preparation expressed by the FEU, which gives more generous scope to individual aspirations for progression than envisaged by the original government proposals (*NTI*, Dec. 1981 Govt).

The 'new curriculum' in this respect provides not only for progression to a job or further or new unemployment, but also a basis for further vocational training or education. The FEU concept of level 2 progression could be established as an aspect of the 'new curriculum', while personal and life skills development seems to be affirmed significant place in the core, along with occupational skills developed from the common core. The influence of the FEU on the 'new curriculum' has been significant and is likely to remain so. Indeed, its early formative influence should not be underestimated. However, the depth or penetration of its influence to what actually happens to trainees in YTS curriculum organizations is subject to several variables. Perhaps the most important of these is to do with the scope of its influence. It can and does communicate its view of the YTS 'new curriculum' to the overall operation in terms of its general influence on the MSC. However, the degree to which this penetrates to the operational level is mediated by the political circumstances of the MSC, and indeed the FEU itself, as a quasi-governmental agency headed by a political appointee. The fact that the FEU view is mediated by the bureaucratic processes of a huge institution (the MSC) and is therefore importantly subject to the usual absorption (sponge-effect) process of the kind familiar to any organization theorist, will limit penetration in any case. Added to these limiting processes is the salience of the 'non-educationalist' view of what the YTS is about within the MSC structures. These fall into two broad kinds, the 'industrialist' view of skills and the 'manpower policy' view of skills-for-employment (if not simply jobs). However, FE is within the direct scope of the FEU via college administrators and also direct to teachers. There is some evidence that penetration can succeed in getting right to the 'chalk-face' by these routes. But there is no less an impression that penetration to this depth is often mediated by LEA structures, which may or may not be sympathetic, depending on, for example, the political and resourcing philosophy of the controlling political group.

The 'new curriculum' will probably have major orientation to pass/fail certification, somewhat ameliorated by the broader positive information base created about a trainee by certification using profiling, with, too, a prospect of this information being negotiated between the certifiers and the trainee. Involved with this latter process is the probable reflexion into the curriculum of a relationship between trainees and teachers which is at once one of closeness and trust associated with guidance/counselling behaviours, while, at the same time, one of monitorial authority in teachers obliged to profile trainees against pass or fail standards, which assure the 'quality' of the training to the 'public' and to an inspectorial external supervision. However, the standards associated with resourcing through funding are likely to be strategically undermined, at least during the introductory phase of YTS as a whole. It is clear that teachers will need considerable relaxation of 'contact hours' to enable them to perform the detailed administration, organization, and development of courses which is most assuredly going to be needed for the effective delivery of the 'new curriculum' at the 'chalk-face'. Added to this, teachers will have to bear a heavy burden of counselling on a one-to-one basis leading to carefully thought out guidance, as well as the generation of detailed records about individual trainees. The argument that teachers involved with TEC and BEC in further education have already adapted to such increase in administrative load is simplistic, and bears the usual hallmarks of FE advisors and managers used to congregating in technically profound advisory committees, which often seem as remote as sky-labs to working teachers. Back on earth, TEC and BEC teachers will pour out their hearts to anyone showing the remotest interest in the intense conflicts over the use of time they invariably face term after term. If the argument is that teachers will *somehow* manage, then, of course, that is a truism of stunning incomprehension.

It must be apparent to even the most ignorant assessment of teachers' work that all these factors, in compound with variously able and motivated trainee groups, cannot fail to create significantly stressful teaching situations. And if, as seems likely, the politics of funding is played out on what could be commonly termed 'a chicken' basis between the MSC (government), the DES and some LEAs, and between LEAs and their institutions, then teachers face a prospect of severe uncertainty about both their prospects in the YTS and their conditions of service. With the MSC in control, and in this respect the Department of Employment and its Secretary of State, the LEAs and the ever competitive Department of Education and Science will fight tooth and nail to the last drop of teachers' blood to negotiate a degree of control commensurate with the proportion of YTS costs 'education' is to subsidize.

'New curriculum' organizations, then, are likely to generate stressed and uncertain teachers, many of whom will be on *very* unfamiliar territory, trying to cope with apparently 'low' level trainees in an extraordinarily complex structure, yet be bound to individualized relations with each trainee. Teachers also face the problem, wholly unexplored to date, of extensive and detailed *public* profiling. In this they have to face the prospect of trainee and parental scrutiny of every adjective used and 'grade' given. This pressure will be juxtaposed with their natural desire to run 'successful' courses and to meet 'inspectorial' scrutiny. The severity of this problem has been either completely underestimated, or left to rest on the inevitable tendency for such profiles to normalize around the bottom half and reduce themselves to mere testimonials of little general currency.

The birth of the 'new curriculum' could well prove traumatic for all concerned, not least for the trainees and their teachers. Yet, it represents a major hope for a long argued for radical reform of the English educational system, in spite of inauspicious beginnings. It resides, however, in a difficult world of factious interests and some-times startling atavism.

> Upon speedy provision of elementary education depends our industrial prosperity. It is no use trying to give technical teaching to our artisans without elementary education; unedu-cated labourers – and many of our labourers are utterly uneducated – are, for the most part, unskilled, notwithstanding their strong sinews and determined energy, they will become over-matched in the competition of the world. Upon this speedy provision depends also, I fully believe, the good, the safe working of our constitutional system. (Forster, W.E., 1870, in Maclure, 1979, p. 104)

But, a skills-based curriculum with a relevant vocational focus often provides the right kind of stimuli for the young person to experience the wider aims of education' (FEU, Nov. 1982, p. 1, para. 4).

Well, the MSC and government do have the independent initiative of the LEAs and the FE system led by the FEU as a counter-balance, even if they do control the purse strings, '. . . that my ploughboy should be taught Greek at the expense of the ratepayer. What then?' (question from the Master of the Rolls during the Cockerton Appeal, in Eaglesham, 1956, p. 126). What then, indeed?

4   *Progression*

Implicit throughout, of course, is the notion that education, as far as the secondary stage at any rate, is unitary and indivisible. Explicitly rejected is the basic dualist ideology of different aims for 'the able' and 'the rest' which has legitimated the bipartite system, still dying a slow and painful death, prolonged by the upturn of the fortunes of its political advocates in the 1970 election. This sytem has defined for most of us our experience of secondary education. 'The able' accounted for some twenty-five per cent of the population – including most of those who grew up to read books like this. For them secondary education followed a pattern that had changed very little for the past century. For the others, four out of five people in the country, secondary schooling was a rudimentary and watered-down version of the same fare. Behind compulsory education for the mass of the people was a simple thought: they ought to be mechanically literate, computationally numerate and politically stable. That was the great social benefit of popular education: it was a benefit rather selectively enjoyed.

Holly, 1973, pp. 9–10

This chapter addresses the 'new curriculum' in terms of the problem of progression. In its first form, related to the original government proposal (*NTI*, Dec. 1981, Govt), trainee progression was very limited. The YTS internal objects seemed to assume trainees would progress simply to jobs in virtue of their improved employability. This simplistic notion of progression remains one aim of the YTS 'new curriculum', but additional and alternative aims were negotiated in the ensuing debate between MSC, government and the institutions, with the views of the FEU gaining ground to a major extent. Emergence of the FEU concept of progression was traced and identified in Chapter 3. As a result of the general debate, intimations of a sophisticated YTS curriculum for vocational preparation included an extended range of individual progression possibilities for trainees. Figure 3 in Chapter 3 illustrates these. However, it is, perhaps, worth re-emphasizing that the FEU view of the 'new curriculum', while fortunately influential, is neither the only influence, nor even a guarantee of, particular practice in FE colleges where LEAs may supply off-the-job training, or are themselves Managing Agencies. In the case of the expected substantial provision through private (non-LEA) Managing Agencies, then FEU influence may, in reality, be significantly diluted; especially in relation to the liberalization of the 'new curriculum', in its FEU guise of 'the changing concept of skill', and the concepts of transferability and trainee ownership of skills. Important as these are, and in spite of MSC/FEU joint statements on curriculum design and implementation, delivery of such significant developments, in the short term at least, is somewhat doubtful.

In summary, and taking this into account, YTS 'new curriculum' organizations could exhibit the following progression behaviours. Each progression leads eventually to the labour market, or is mediated by the market. Trainees could proceed to further skills training on a full-time basis, or, through employment, on a part-time basis in a college of further education. Alternatively, trainees could proceed to further vocational education on a full-time basis, or, through employment, on a part-time basis in a college of further education. Or, trainees may gain employment which includes training through an employer's own training scheme provided by the employer directly. Or, trainees could proceed in an extension of the YTS for further vocational preparation. Or, trainees could enter employment which does not provide further training or education. Lastly, trainees could leave their YTS for simple unemployment.

Included in this summary is the distinct prospect of some trainees 'progressing' to further or new unemployment. In this respect it is worth noting a distinction between outcomes and progression of considerable, if obvious, social significance. An outcome which in-volves the trainee only in further or new unemployment clearly could not (and should not) be regarded as a form of progression. The 'new curriculum', consequently, does not overtly aim to prepare trainees for unemployment, but to prepare them for progression. There is certainly substantial labour market evidence to support those who advocate including preparation for coping with unemployment in YTS courses. Such coping-skills training is treated pejoratively by those who argue that the whole scheme is reduceable to a politically cynical cosmetic or statistics massaging exercise. Indeed, many who see the logic of such 'coping' training being included in the 'new curriculum' are sensitive to the charge that they could be running 'unemployment courses', or that the schemes are merely 'training for unemployment'. The simple unemployment outcome is included in the above summary of possible progressions in the understanding that, so far as the YTS 'new curriculum' is concerned, there is no clear or overt aim to prepare trainees to cope with unemployment, such an outcome not being regarded as progress. It goes without saying that the social stigma attached to the unemployment outcome for those who will inevitably 'fail to progress' could be very great indeed in their own perception.

It can be seen immediately that all except this last outcome can be regarded as progress for the individual trainee, and such progress includes a job without further education and training. This latter progression is of a very simple kind in keeping with one of the government's initial main objectives, which was to provide a scheme which would make trainees simply employable. Obviously, while the employability of each trainee is itself a factor in whether they compete successfully for a job, the present inherent mismatch between vacancies and applicants is not solved by improving the general quality of the applicants, as discussed in Chapter 2. It was indicated in Chapter 3 that trainees would be certified using a profiling scheme which could in effect grade each trainee, and could have a major pass/fail implication. It was intimated that differentiation would be an inherent aspect of the 'new curriculum' in terms of this process. It is clear what the purpose of this differentiation process could be, other than the provision of a profile certificate for employers (and trainees themselves) giving them, among other things, a hierarchic indication of the comparative performance of each trainee. Such certification could, too, provide a basis for selecting trainees for other progression into full-time further education.

It is at once apparent that the outcomes for trainees of their YTS courses can be, and are likely to be, seen in hierarchic terms. Figure 6 illustrates such a hierarchy in a tentative manner. It is not possible, of course, to express a definitive view at this stage, because YTS courses have not yet been run, except in pilot schemes, and there is little actual experience of the 'new curriculum' as such. The upper reaches of Figure 6 are optimistic, in terms of being progressions realistically open to

Figure 6.   A Tentative Hierarchy of the Outcomes of YTS Courses

Highest level . . . . Employment with vocational education/
training for a professional qualification

Full-time vocational education/training for a
professional qualification

Employment with further skill training for
craft/technician qualification

Full-time further skill training for a craft/
technician qualification

Further full-time skill training MSC special
scheme

Employment without further
education/training

Extension of YTS

Lowest level . . . . Unemployment

YTS leavers. Nevertheless, Figure 6 does represent a commonsense extrapolation adduced from such work as has been done by the Standing Conference of Regional Advisory Councils for Further Education (SCRACFE, 1980) and the FEU (Jan. 1981, *Signposts,*), among others. It is noticeable that the 'new curriculum' clearly does not provide for progression to the traditional scholastic examination system of O- and A-level GCE. In this respect the FEU's analysis of the context of vocational preparation for 16–19-year-olds holds good (Jan. 1981, Vocational Preparation section 11), and provides a key to the starting point of this analysis.

Before outlining the FEU analysis it is worth mentioning its essential weakness, and indeed a common weakness of much educational writing, that of 'fudge'. The fudge is essentially associated with a failure to admit the reality that vocational preparation courses are *in effect* a provision for the less bright, that is, the bottom 40 per cent. By this is meant those 16-year-olds who cannot succeed in passing any

O-level GCEs or CSEs in order to advance into the sixth form 'university and professional' stream, or to find employment with 'prospects', which must mean further education and training. Such pupils have theoretically shared in *the* common curriculum of secondary schools, but have, in practice, spent much of their time being led to the 'watered-down version' of the fare of the able, as it was put by Douglas Holly (1973), and referred to as the 'other curriculum' in this book. Admittedly, 'fudge' is somewhat too pejorative of the FEU's sensitivity to the broad issue. Nevertheless, there is a tendency for the issue to be obfuscated by an oversubtle concentration on the long-term objective to reform the system as a whole, the introduction of vocational preparation and recognition of experiential learning being conducive to this end.

Figure 7 (extracted from FEU, Jan. 1981, *Vocational Preparation*, 9) illustrates the structure of existing provision and the place of vocational preparation. It can be seen that the 'new curriculum' fits the route (iii) vocational preparation area and is likely to replace the variety of schemes which presently come under this head. Reference to Figure 8 shows route (iii), now simplified by the provision of YTSs based on the 'new curriculum'. The negotiated curriculum of vocational preparation in Figure 7 becomes the 'new curriculum' which still retains some

Figure 7. Categorization (FEU) of Existing Education and Training Provision Related to Conventional Intelligence or Capability

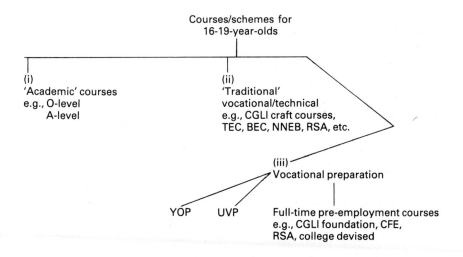

Source: FEU, Jan, 1981, p. 9, section 11.

Figure 8.   Categorization (FEU) by Source of Curricula

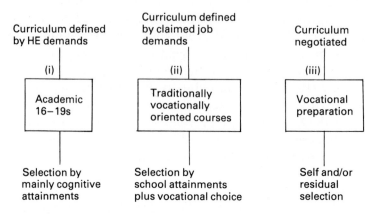

Source: FEU, Jan. 1981, p. 9, section 11.

negotiated content, but within the limits of the range of skills related to occupational families. In this sense the 'new curriculum' is defined by 'claimed job demands' in the way of traditional vocationally oriented courses, except that the syllabus and standards are not laid down by the present range of external validating bodies, but will emerge from or through the MSC.

Figure 9 illustrates the effective relationship of the 'new curriculum' to existing provision, taking into account its tentative hierarchy of outcomes and the concept of progression through selection. The word 'brightness' is used somewhat crudely, but there is little doubt that common perception is somewhat crude and to this point. This is simply recognized here, but not, of course, taken as educationally significant, except in so far as common perceptions are immensely influential in the formation of attitudes about the status of courses and qualifications – a point no educationalist can overlook with impunity. The continuing problem of currency affecting the CSE is a case in point.

Figure 8 shows that the 'new curriculum' does not provide a significant or deliberate route to higher education except by the most tortuous process. In particular, it positively excludes trainees from non-vocational studies which could connect with O- and/or A-level work. This would include, too, the science Os and As as non-vocational studies, although certain of the new Os and As could relate (such as computer studies); however, there is no indication whatsoever that trainees could acquire either a basis for traditional qualification or

Figure 9. The Relationship of the 'New Curriculum' to Existing Provision for 16–19-Year-Olds Showing the Hierarchic Nature of Outcomes and Progressions (from left to right)

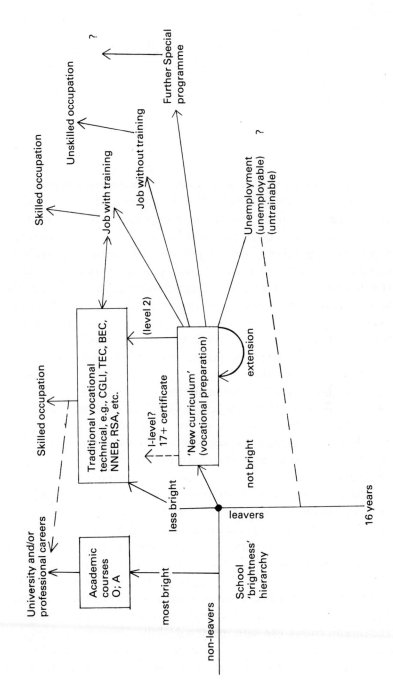

the qualifications directly. While these remain the key route to higher education and the professions, and in spite of continuing debate, this seems certain to remain the case, the 'new curriculum' is assuredly almost impeccably nineteenth century in its potential for socio-economic segmentation. Admittedly, since those days the problem of access has been ameliorated, although not by any means eradicated. Consequently, the effect is largely to institutionalize early individual differences within the education system in terms of a labour market philosophy based less on the realities of that market than on political beliefs about the rightful order of things.

Although major arguments for the reform of entry to higher education, and indeed the reform of higher education itself, *seem* to be gaining ground, entrenchment is so deep as to make this very unlikely, even in the medium term. The key point, then, is that the 'new curriculum' is likely to be a component of the present quasi-meritocratic status quo, although seen by many as a potential instrument, among others, in the pressure for reform, particularly *if* its certification could ever demonstrably acquire social and instrumental status equal to traditional, accepted, forms. Its 'fit' into the quasi-meritocratic status quo incorporates all the social divisions encompassed therein, as demonstrated by (among others) Floud, Halsey and Martin (1957), Le-Grand (1982, Chapter 4), Holly (1973) and somewhat brutally exposed by Young *et al.* (1971) and Young and Whitty (1976, 1977).

It could be argued that provision of communications with life and personal skills in the 'new curriculum' is somehow like the general studies of yesteryear. This provision could be seen to provide an opportunity to establish some basis of O-level preparation for trainees, giving them an option on leaving to enter, or progress to, a traditional combination of O/A-level examination courses, if they so desired. Assuming such individualization of the 'new curriculum' is operationally feasible, and indeed practised, then some trainees could receive significant preparation along such lines. However, progression of this sort is clearly ruled out so far as the aims of the 'new curriculum' are concerned and, indeed, so far as the controlling agency, the MSC (DOE), is concerned. In the simplest terms, the 'new curriculum' could be locally manipulated for some individual trainees to progress to the higher education route on the basis of an individually expanded communications/life and personal skills element, although such an outcome is clearly not sought by the government and MSC, nor is this likely to be contemplated by employers operating Managing Agencies and buying in off-the-job training from the FE sector. The point here is that the 'new curriculum' is fundamentally preventative of such an outcome. The FEU connives in this because it disapproves, in any case, of higher education defined curricula. Nevertheless, the socio-economic differentiation associated with the present system of routes to occupations cannot be overlooked in respect of the 'new curriculum' simply because the curricula associated with the main route to power and superior economic benefit in society are disapproved of by the FEU (and others). There is little doubt that social and life skills training has little or no connection with a serious attempt to resurrect the socio-economic prospects of low attainment trainees, beyond schooling them for a disciplined role at the bottom of the jobs hierarchy or quiescence on the dole.

It would be naive to assume the FEU's broader strategy for reform does not include aspirations for the status of the 'new curriculum', and it is noteworthy that it has argued strongly for major linkage between 'experiential learning' and any new 17+ certification (I-level).

> ... we believe it is possible to improve this situation (of 'intellectual apartheid') by a new 17+ curriculum which deliberately bridges the schism that exists between education and training by openly declaring that it will satisfy the criteria of vocational preparation ...

> This means some recognition of experiential learning and we see no reason why any new 17+ certification should not include the accreditation of planned experience. (FEU, Dec. 1981, *Progressing from Vocational Preparation*, para. 12)

Whether this refers to the 17+ vocational preparation or the now defunct I-level proposals is not clear. Presumably, the FEU wanted experiental learning recognized in the context of a system of 17+ examination which followed on from the 16+ structure and consequentially reformed it.

The 'new curriculum' could be seen, therefore, as a basis for influencing 17+ certification, displacing the influence of present HE defined curricula. Presumably 17+ certification could in this sense be seen as a stage of qualification for higher education as well as further vocational education and training. Such thinking has resulted in, and typifies, the false consensus that has sprung up between the most unlikely groupings in relation to the emergence of the YTS 'new curriculum'. Notwithstanding this, the 'new curriculum', in the context of the present state of the educational system, cannot be seen as providing any significant route or opportunity for trainees to progress to higher education, indeed it is *preventative* of such an outcome.

This is to some extent made explicit in the government's (DES) recent statement on a 17+ certificate. Essentially, this putative qualification is seen as one for those 16–19-year-olds who remain in school (full-time education), but are generally unsuited to 'academic' work, that is, O and A-level courses leading to examination. Trainees in YTS are not to take the new examination (Pre-Vocational Leaving Certificate, PVLC), but to continue with the proposed profile certification for YTSs. The statement (DES and Welsh Office, May 1982, *17+: A New Certificate*) goes on to maintain, throughout, the distinction between education and training, and it is quite apparent that this reflects the deep strategic clash between the DES and DOE. In any case, what is clear is that the government sees the new certificate in terms of an 'instead of' policy and not as a replacement for a combined O- and CSE-level certification. In this sense, the PVLC certificate is likely to be very much a second best, and not prove to be the revolutionary all embracing certification for a raised leaving age school population. Where YTS profile certificates end up in status terms is discussed later.

Before dealing with the main element of this chapter, the exploration and analysis of 'official' progression, it is important to deal with the related issue of allowances. This issue is related both to the preceding conclusion that the 'new curriculum' *design* prevents progression to HE defined curricula, and to the notion that allowances are an aspect of it too. This is to say that progression of any kind can be prevented in four ways. First, by effective non or negative linkage in curricular terms between the 'new curriculum' and other curricula, such as HE defined curricula. Secondly, is by regulation/validation. This would be to prevent progression simply by making and/or using regulations to prevent linkage, for example, that a 'pass' profile certificate is not an entry qualification for certain courses of further training or education, thus preventing entry by specific exclusion of that particular qualification, that is, whoever holds only this certificate will in virtue of the regulation be specifically excluded from entry. Thirdly, and perhaps together with the second, to leave the status of the profile certification undeclared, but open to speculation and subject to popular, or institutionally and/or politically planned debasement or enhancement, depending on the 'interests' of the bodies concerned. Lastly, prevention of 'progress' can be established through two kinds of funding controls: personal allowances to trainees and course support; and also, or separately, sponsorship of providing organizations in terms of their costs. Involved with this latter aspect is control of the permission to run or mount courses, particularly significant in further education and associated with the powers of LEAs and the DES.

Progression, then, is potentially subject to any of these instruments singly or in combination. Such instruments are highly susceptible to the political objectives of the various, to use a systems term, 'actors' in the educational system. Such objectives are of an ideological or interest kind, variously and changeably distributed in the system. Consequently, progression through the 'new curriculum' is likely to be subject to a complex, ambiguous, even confused set of preventions and inducements.

On the matter of allowances in particular, it was established in Chapter 3 that there is presently only scope for trainees to be supported for one year, and then *only* in a MSC backed YTS scheme. Certainly, there is pressure for a review of the question of allowances in respect of all 16-19-year-olds in full-time education, but this is exceedingly tentative and unlikely to proceed at any pace relevant to the short or medium-term future. Changes in this respect will finally depend entirely on which political party forms the next government. What does seem possible at this time, is that certain trainees could receive longer-term support. This is significant to the concept of progression through the 'new curriculum', particularly in relation to the question of selection. It seems possible that the MSC could be encouraged to broaden the scope of its funding of allowances to individual trainees, in terms of both special (further) skill training programmes, and also through a kind of discretionary funding of individual trainees' progression to relevant further education. What is of central importance to the 'new curriculum' is that progression of these kinds is placed very effectively in the hands controlling the purse strings of the individual trainee, namely the MSC (DOE) and the Secretary of State for Employment; one can only note the relapse of the DES and the Secretary of State for Education. One is tempted to speculate about the grave view Robert Morant might take of this unravelling of his great knitting together of 1902, but this would be to digress.

That aside, it can be concluded that trainee progression to relevant further education and training is, materially under the influence of the MSC. Quite clearly, selection for such support will take place and be based on the performance of the trainee on the YTS course. This will be measured and assessed throughout the course, and be presented in terms of the profile certificate 'awarded' at the end of the course. The certificates, in this sense, could turn out to have real 'currency', besides being complicated public 'references' for potential employers. What is clear about the 'new curriculum' is that its certification process could be materially vital to individual trainees' prospects of progression not only in respect of selection for employment, but also in respect of selection for further training or education.

The term 'progression' can now be seen to be synonymous with advancement. Profile certificates could largely determine the advancement of trainees. They can advance themselves by performing well in the process of the 'new curriculum', they can get a good result. A good result may enable them to advance in terms of the upper reaches of the tentative hierarchy of outcomes shown in Figure 6. However, and this is where the uneasy alliance between the MSC and FEU crumbles somewhat, the prospect of funding for trainees to advance to further full-time vocational education and training is, at present, dim. What seems to be in the offing, as already stated, is funding for one-year special skill training programmes, or an extension of YTS. Consequently, while trainee advancement is possible in terms of the hierarchy, actual prospects of *progression* to courses in the upper level of the hierarchy are limited. This limitation is controlled by the MSC (and government). Advancement to such a level will therefore largely depend on the trainee succeeding in the competition for jobs with release, or facilities, for vocational education and training. It is an obvious point, but must nevertheless be made, that such jobs are usually reserved for high O-level leavers, or later leavers with A-levels. Indeed, the entry regulations to many *professional* courses leading to professional qualifications require significant O- and/or A-level entry qualifications. The I-level concept of the FEU might have eventually lessened this difficulty if experiential learning had been legitimated in its curriculum, however I-level in this sense is now defunct.

In summary, three preventative factors operate against trainees advancing to the higher levels of the outcomes hierarchy: the MSC's (apparent) funding policy; entry regulations to such courses; and employers' perception of the comparative status of traditional qualifications and the YTS profile certificates. It can be readily appreciated, therefore, that progression in practice is restricted to the lower levels of the Figure 6 tentative hierarchy of outcomes, which may broadly be described as craft level progressions. Advancement then is effectively limited to employment and/or further skill training at craft level, or unskilled employment without training and unemployment. It is of great importance in consideration of the 'new curriculum' that these de facto limitations (preventions) are not only recognized, but recognized as limitations sustained by policy considerations lodged deep in the broad establishment (not only this government), and not simply derived in the 'accidents' of the way the present 'system' of 16–19 education has come about. Not to do so would be to underestimate entirely the depth to which the present system has become socially and politically entrenched. It is worthy of note that 'the establishment' referred to assumes in its breadth such diverse echelons of power and influence as trade union leaderships and the governments of universities, as well as the obviously conservative institutions.

Such definite narrowing of progression presumes a certain national manpower policy, involving (inextricably) certain social assumptions about the future role in society of a major proportion of 16–19-year-olds, based on their secondary school performance, as measured by the O and A system. The 'new curriculum' is actually *preventative* of those whose performance has actually failed to measure up in this traditional way from progressing outside the narrow band of outcomes just stated. Certainly, this is an improvement in the range of prospects open to those leavers who at one time were absorbed into the unskilled and semi-skilled labour market, and are presently faced with unemployment because of both the economic recession and the changing structure of demand; both demand deficient and structural unemployment, as discussed in Chapter 2. However, it was noted there that many traditional manual craft skills would not be required in the context of a resurgence in demand.

Graham Markell's (1982) criticism of the MSC's job creation programme was not without justice when referring to the common-sense of working-class boys about their transition to work and eager escape from the state education system.

> In so doing they effectively (though not self consciously) see through the false premise or empty promise of formal educational/vocational achievement in a labour market characterised by a competitive system of entry. For if they were all to complete 'some form of vocational training' (just as if they were all to gain CSE, O or A levels) then that would not offer any assurance of a job (even MSC has to recognise this) but simply 'up' the terms of competition for whatever jobs were available – jobs whose number and nature is determined by the 'pull' of the market and not by the 'push' of the attributes

(educational or otherwise) of their potential incumbents. (Markell, 1982, p. 94)

However, he treats unemployment in terms of simple demand deficiency and, in consequence, does not embrace the broader implications of a future labour market pulling employment into a changed structure. The manpower policy fear is that such pull will suffer serious strain caused by the inevitable resistance of a supply-side pool of uneducated, unskilled, alienated and disenchanted long-term unemployed *people*, unable or disinclined to rise to the challenge of new-skill jobs.

It was argued in Chapter 3 that the ability range of YTS trainees may be wider than might be expected, because the presumption that able minimum age leavers will be selected for jobs and the less able will not, hardly applies in the present highly depressed youth labour market. The implications of such depression include the distinct possibility that a significant proportion of minimum age leavers would 'normally' have found jobs which included further education and training, had such jobs continued in the labour market. Such leavers may indeed have traditional qualifications suited to such progression through a 'normal' employment situation. The question of 'normality' returning is a difficult one explored in Chapter 2. At this stage, it is sufficient to recognize that the ability range of minimum age leavers displaced from the labour market by the present situation is likely to include some leavers capable of progression to the higher levels of the tentative hierarchy of outcomes in Figure 6. The 'new curriculum' could prevent their advancement to such levels, even if ability streaming can (should) be mounted by YTS providing organizations. Such trainees will be left to compete, presumably successfully, for what progression there is in the 'new curriculum' by forming either the 'top' stream, or the top passers in mixed ability classes. Selection for advancement (progression) could be based on their profile certificates and previous traditional qualifications, and be dependent upon the results of the MSC's control policy on the flow (rate, numbers and kind) of trainees into further training for occupational skills, and upon employers' needs, expressed through their individual recruitment and training policies.

In addition to all these points about the nature of progression through the 'new curriculum' is the matter of the strategic realignment of the status of vocational preparation, and consequently the status of the YTS profile certificates. This, as already discussed, involves the broad modification of entry requirements to 'level 2' so that YTS profile certificates can at least exempt trainees from level 1. As some YTS trainees may have entered such courses in normal times, and, in any case, could be drawn to YTSs by the personal allowances involved, such realignment seems both feasible and likely. Such change is made more likely if it is indeed the case that many able minimum age leavers will not have 'normal' access to jobs which enable such further education and training. Selection for such progression would therefore permit some trainees to be supported by the MSC, on the basis of their YTS performance as measured by the profile certificates. While this is an obvious pragmatism, it should not be overlooked that it is a strategic development in both the funding of college students through the 'first year' of traditional courses, and in the fundamental status of the 'new curriculum' in relation to traditional (or normal) vocational/technical provision. In this sense it would be a general 'prep' course with personal allowances.

There is some possibility, too, of the profile certificates becoming 'equivalent' to a new 17+ certificate. Such a development would lead to a major interaction between the two certification processes and perhaps conclude with the 17+ certificate being much like a YTS profile certificate. The present DES argument for their separation would inevitably dissolve as a consequence, leaving one certificate for pre-vocational preparation, a PVPC, whether applicable to 17+ school leavers or YTS leavers. The real difficulty in this lies in the gulf between the present government's populist objective of sustaining a modified O- and A-level GCE and CSE unified system (as satisfying the 'standards and traditions' argument) and the 17+ certificate acting as an I-level *replacement* for HE defined examination, with strategic implications for the secondary school curriculum. Such change is not envisaged, but would paradoxically meet a key proposition of the Secretaries of State for Education and Science, and Wales, about secondary education. This is the third proposition they wished to emphasize about secondary education in *The School Curriculum* (March 1981).

> School education needs to equip young people fully for adult and working life in a world which is changing very rapidly indeed, particularly in consequence of new technological developments: they must be able to see where their education has meaning outside school. (DES and Welsh Office, March 1981, para. 39.3)

However, while this is seen by the Secretaries of State as a vital aspect of secondary education, so is the maintenance of a broad and balanced curriculum pre-16 (*ibid.*, para. 40). Consequently, there would seem to be little real prospect of cramming pre-vocational training into already critically overstuffed timetables. The exception, of course, is those low ability 14-year-olds who are not expected to manage 'real' examination courses. It is quite contrary, of course, to DES and apparently government objectives, for only low ability 14-year-olds to be equipped for adult and working life. There is the strong and influential belief that all 14–16s should participate in a broad, balanced common curriculum, until minimum school leaving age, when those who 'fail' to mount the traditional hurdles may either leave, or now may continue in school on a pre-vocational preparation course leading to the new 17+ certificate. With sufficient lead preparation, and modification to the curriculum during the 14–16 period, all pupils could participate in pre-vocational training, and continue to the new 'examination' (or certification), while not necessarily being precluded by such preparation from engaging in the traditional examination scheme. Consequently, A-level students could achieve, as well, a 17+ pre-vocational leaving certificate, while others could add this to O-levels before leaving, while others could leave at 17 with no other certificates except this.

However, government policy on the 17+ certificate (DES and Welsh Office, May 1982, para. 12), as pointed out in Chapter 2, excludes all but the latter from its target group. The proposed Certificate of Pre-Vocational Education (CPVE) seems set to emerge as a kind of school YTS certificate for the less bright, and has little to do with reforming the examination system and the common curriculum, or with the concept for reform behind the FEU's perception of the defunct I-level proposals (counting experiential learning as part of qualification). The government's New Training and Vocational Education Initiative (NTVEI) seems set to provide a long-term means of modifying the secondary school curriculum in terms of generating a vocational emphasis from 14+ for all pupils. Consequently, the secondary curriculum is likely to formally bifurcate at 14 on the basis of 'ability'. Low attainment 14-year-olds will get a YTS type of curriculum, the 'new curriculum', the top 60 per cent will get a more vocationally oriented GCSE dominated curriculum. The NTVEI is intended to deliberalize the subject structure and content of the secondary school curriculum, making it 'more relevant to the needs of industry'. This is broadly in line with the Macfarlane Report (Dec. 1980, para. 46) and conforms to the tenor of the Oct. 1980 consultative paper, *Examinations 16–18*, of the Secretaries of State for Education and Science. It fits, too, with the proposal for a unified GCE O-level and CSE 16+ examination (DES and Welsh Office, Nov. 1982). This 'General Certificate of Secondary Education' (GCSE) is a provision for the top half (60 per cent) and the CPVE is for the bottom half (40 per cent).

> The new examinations (GCSE) and their syllabuses must be capable of meeting the diverse needs of all candidates in the top sixty per cent range of ability in each subject among pupils of sixteen-plus. The examination would be open to all who wish to take it but the syllabuses and assessment procedures would be designed in order to reward the attainment of pupils spanning the whole range of ability in the school population. The examination would provide a certificate of achievement for those leaving full-time education at sixteen-plus, as well as a basis for further study and for entry into training. (DES and Welsh Office, Nov. 1982, p. 3)

It also interestingly, and perhaps paradoxically, reflects the view of the FEU (Jan. 1981, *Vocational Preparation*, para. 14, and later):

> This cohort does not form a simple target group with easily identifiable coherent and shared characteristics. It would be possible to identify sub-groups within the cohort, but this would be a spurious solution. It is more constructive to explore for this group common curricular approaches which suit them rather than design a series of set courses into which learners are then fitted. (FEU, Jan. 1981, *Vocational Preparation*, para. 30)

Surely, these less bright pupils will be intrigued by any coincidence between the 17+ level certificate and the YTS profile certificate, especially when a personal allowance is payable in a YTS and not, at present, for continuing in school. Such coincidence would be particularly happy in the unlikely event that YTSs provided significant progression/advancement on a planned, well organized and possibly supported basis. It is plain that the present DES and Welsh Office position on the 17+ certificate is fraught with the prospect of a tough division of interest between the MSC's control of YTS and the DES's attempt to retain control of 17+ certification. The division is once more based on distinction between training and education. A pre-vocational curriculum with 17+ certification in schools is education, the YTS 'new curriculum', dominated by work experience and profile certification, is training. It is plain that the formation of one certificate as indicated by the FEU is political oil and water in spite of its obvious curricular logic. That one certificate should inescapably emerge, in this latter sense, could be in any case prevented by the interest in government of avoiding the cost of extending the coverage of YTS by the (inevitable) inducement of personal allowances, beyond political and labour market expediency.

There is serious confusion, therefore, about the *level* of the 17+ certificate, compounded by the impression that YTS vocational preparation will somehow be an even lower level of course than the new certificate will require. Perhaps it will include experiential learning, but yet cover more 'advanced' areas of pre-vocational preparation? Such confusion is obviously unnecessary in terms of curriculum design, but necessary to the battle of the two interests aiming to control the respective education/training arenas. The present government may be content to ensure that pre-vocational preparation through the expensive YTS can be gradually withdrawn in favour of 17+ certification in schools linked with an informal raising of the school leaving age.

Figure 10 attempts a closer summary of the possible range of transitions from 14–16 HE oriented secondary curricula to 16–19 curricula, than given by Figure 9. It shows the school objective of providing all 14–16s with a broad, balanced, common curriculum leading to the minimum leaving age transition point when an increasing proportion of pupils face some form of examination. Progression depends largely on expected or predicted results subject to modification by actual performance. The putative position of YTS in the hierarchy of school outcomes is plain. It is potentially a separate path of perhaps remedial training and social schooling for low ability or attainment minimum age leavers in the YOP ethos. If YTS remains isolated from the overall educational system and 14–19 schemes of curricula, it is likely to realize such a potential, easily becoming little more than a low status alternative to 'proper' training and education provided by schools and FE colleges in the traditional framework.

Quite clearly, the question of whether YTS courses will lead to the same qualifications as school provided pre-vocational 'education' is a significant one. Separation of the 17+ certificate from the YTS profile certificates, no matter how narrowly sustained in real curriculum terms, will contribute to such isolation. Progression for YTS trainees will be less viable in so far as profile certificates are likely to take up a status position at the bottom of the qualifications hierarchy. This would be particularly induced by a 17+ certificate forming part of a

*Figure 10.   A Tentative Hierarchy: 14–16 Progression to 17+ Certification
(I-Level in School?) and Minimum Age Leavers' Progression to YTS*

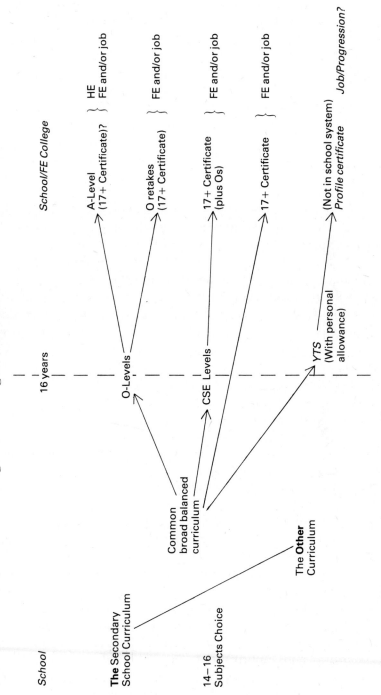

mix of GCSEs and A-levels for the upper attainment range of pupils. This is to say that the status of a 17+ certificate could be enhanced, by association, in a mix with traditional (that is, publicly accepted) qualifications. It is not clear whether the 'new curriculum' will be permitted integral status with a new 17+ pre-vocational leaving course undertaken within the schools system. Separation is likely to be attractive to interests wishing to avoid extrapolation of personal allowances into the post-16 full-time education system. If the DES succeeds in artificially isolating YTS vocational preparation, the overall prospects of progression for YTS trainees will tend to reduce. As already delineated above, even without such isolation, progression will in any case be extremely limited.

Nevertheless, the further education system is likely to 'make do' with YTS profile certificates, thus enabling a proportion of YTS trainees to continue in traditional FE if at all possible. This is likely because it is in the interest of the FE sector to supplement its declining catchment of students; it has a significant record for this kind of survival (or entrepreneurialism). As a result, progression within FE provision is not likely to be obstructed by an over zealous local admissions policy in respect of the profile certification, provided, of course, trainees actually wish to progress without support, as if they were re-entering full-time education. It should be noted here that the 21-hour option, whereby the unemployed could remain qualified for supplementary benefit and yet undertake a course leading to a recognized qualification in an FE college, has been subject to serious obstruction through deliberate administrative regulation by the Department of Health and Social Security. The obvious implication is that unemployed young people are being directed away from their interests and away from freely choosing courses in further education generally, and toward the YTS only, with its structure of preventions against significant progression, and its capacity for schooling the bottom half.

Figure 11 attempts a summary of the variables affecting YTS trainee progression discussed so far. The scope for individual variables to vary and their interaction has been discussed; but, it can be seen at a glance from Figure 11 that the potential for mere confusion to de-energize the entire process of the 'new curriculum' is very great indeed. Inside this entire complex of variables affecting YTS trainee progression is the individual 16- or 17-year-old with his or her own personality, aims, motivations, friends, family, hopes and fears. This person's individual motivation to 'progress' may very well prove the key factor in the capacity of 'new curriculum' organizations to *provide*

Figure 11. *Schematic Summary of Variables Affecting YTS Progression*

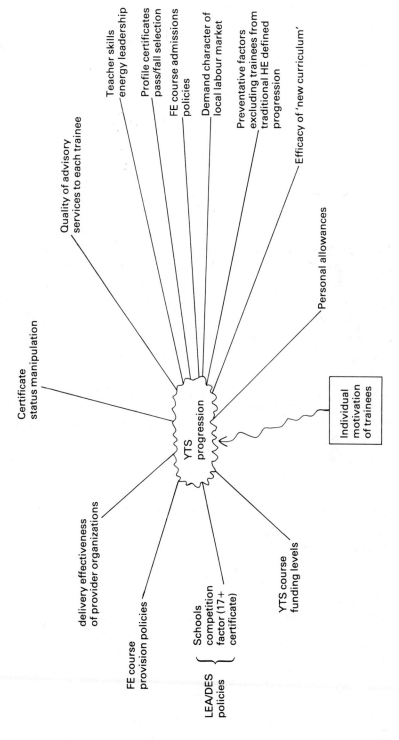

progression even of a limited kind. However, there is a serious chicken and egg problem in this. Treating the 'new curriculum' as organizations in which trainees become members highlights this difficulty. Apart from sociological perspectives which produce arguments that young people are likely to be antipathetic to yet another MSC scheme, there is the actual effect of the behaviour of 'new curriculum' organizations on their members to consider. In this the potential for progression/advancement inherent in the behaviour of curriculum organizations will crucially affect the motivation of their individual members, as will their related perceptions of the value of such progressions. Of course, this is to continue to leave aside predicting whose values will end up with the decisive influence on the definition of progress: trainees, teachers, administrators/managers, employers, MSC, government, the labour market, society. What will happen in practice is that organization norms will form and determine such definition. The formation of organizational norms is an intricate process involving such broad variables as organization structure, practices and social processes.

'New curriculum' organizations, and indeed all curriculum organizations, can be treated in terms of their capacity to motivate individuals to progress. In spite of *all* mediating variables, the aims and motivation of the individual trainee can be thought of as a determining variable. This is to say that whatever else impinges on and affects individual capacity to progress in the 'new curriculum', a trainee who does not want to find a job, for example, will not do so. A low ability trainee highly motivated to find a job may perform comparatively well and find a job, this being mediated by, of course, the variable of local labour market demand characteristics. Obviously, ability is an important factor affecting performance. However the question of ability is a complex one involving the difficult concept of intelligence. Intelligence has been considerably researched in the last forty years, and it remains the subject of considerable debate and scrutiny in philosophical, sociological and psychological terms. However, it is surely a measurable attribute of some kind, bearing on the relative success or failure of individuals in the education system. Nevertheless, level of motivation importantly affects performance, and cannot be overlooked as a major factor in the potential effectiveness of the 'new curriculum'. For example,

> Intelligence is without doubt associated with high achievement
> in a very wide range of tasks and occupations. But even in those

to which it is most directly relevant, it accounts for no more than about half the variation in performance, and in some situations and groups, much less. Educational and applied psychologists are at present deeply concerned with analysing other relevant factors, particularly those associated with level of motivation. (Butcher, 1968, p. 290)

Individual trainee motivation can be crucially associated with the formation of YTS group norms and attitudes. Deeply involved with and affecting this will be the individual influence of YTS teachers springing from their own motivations, attitudes, skills and interests. The nature of the interaction of teachers and trainees in the process of 'new curriculum' organizations is, therefore, of central importance to individual trainee motivation, and motivation is a significant key to trainee progression. Amongst all the variables mediating YTS progression, this interaction occurs at what can be termed the human interface, that is, the interface between trainees and teachers as members of the same curriculum organization. In the final analysis, whatever else mediates YTS progression, there will be real trainees physically with real teachers in one place interacting with each other in terms of both the 'new curriculum' process and their own predilections. It is not unimportant, therefore, to an analysis of YTS progression to consider the human interface, bearing in mind that this aspect of progression is not, of course, simply isolable from the mediating variables shown in Figure 11.

It can be expected that at least some trainees in each discrete YTS group will start out in a mood of disaffection. Their behaviour in particular may easily form the basis of a key group norm, significantly influencing the attitudes and behaviour of the whole group. Prospects of progression (advancement) may, therefore, be perceived in a cynical perspective. Such perception is likely to be reinforced by the fact that progression is uncertain and in any case limited. Prospects of progression are surely closely linked with the 'what's the point of all this' questioning, likely to be in the minds, and in the manner, of trainees as they join the 'new curriculum' process. Add to this the recording/ examining/monitorial/bureaucratic role of teachers, as discussed in Chapter 3, then the possibility of an early entrenchment of a 'them and us' attitude becomes a very distinct one.

Williamson (1980) summary of client responses to YOP draws a useful distinction between professional (-class) teachers and working (-class) supervisors. Essentially, personal relations between trainees and both kinds of staff tended to be good, but the knowledge of working (-class) supervisors was more valued because it seemed connected with real work and therefore jobs. Trainees were interested in progressing to real jobs or 'real' training. Such training was invariably job-specific skill training for craft type jobs. The formal rationale of YOP, as YTS, is preventative of specific craft skill training, at least of sufficient depth and quality to lead to qualification to do a particular job. Professional knowledge about social and life skills had little currency among YOP trainees.

> The operation of firm discipline may be resented at first, but the very real physical dangers of the workplace (for instance, heavy slabs on building sites, or machinery in workshops) soon demonstrates to trainees in a practical way the need for discipline and the unacceptability of 'messing about'. Consequently, the guidance and information offered by 'working class' staff is valued by, and does have an impact on trainees. In contrast, the presentation of sessions on race relations, on 'behaviour at work' or on health and safety in a sterile 'classroom situation' (and anything which does not involve work but is neither unpaid free time is interpreted as 'like school') is detested and generates resentment and opposition. The lack of its direct relevance to a concrete situation militates against its impact. (Williamson, 1982, p. 112)

The controversy over how long trainees should spend doing off-the-job training, thirteen weeks or twenty-six weeks or something in between, might seem irrelevant in terms of Williamson's finding. However, progression to jobs remains an increasingly competitive process for trainees, and, in consequences, their perception of the ultimate advancement through membership of a curriculum organization to a job is likely to remain part of the prospectus of disappointment for many. However, any chance of progression to individual educational development through a 'new curriculum' organization enabling some trainees to enter a vocational FE course leading to 'real' qualification would need a *substantial* amount of off-the-job training and individualized tutorial and guidance resources. The dilemma is obvious and perplexing: maximize the off-the-job training and risk sterile classrooms; or minimize, and lose any real possibility of trainees progressing to further education.

With these points in mind, it is apparent that the work of FE YTS teachers will prove arduous and stressful. The kind of students and the teaching involved are substantially different from the traditional FE pattern. Faced with this, and possibly mixed ability groups, potentially low levels of trainee motivation and behaviour, together with burdensome administration, many lecturers may prefer not to become involved. Added to which the work is graded at the lowest level (5B), by the Burnham Grading of Courses Sub-Committee, with all that implies for lecturers' prospects.

> A revision of the Burnham points system will, however, be necessary if colleges are to seriously consider switching resources from high level to vocational preparation courses, and if teaching of these programmes is to present an attractive career opportunity to lecturers. (SCRACFE, 1980, para. 10.24 ii)

It is noteworthy that most colleges have not exactly considered switching resources, but rather of adding resources to their present operations in keeping with the expansionist traditions of further education.

> Two elements within FE were prepared to help the disadvantaged, unemployed young people. The first were the compassionate the caring principals, vice-principals, heads of departments and lecturers. They often found themselves supported by the second group, the 'empire builders'. These people saw that funds could be obtained for the young unemployed, and that part of those funds could be used to support what some regarded as the 'real' students. Thus, developed the any course/ most profit course syndrome. (Newell, 1982. p. 23)

In a tough and critical article Newell went on to accuse local authorities of raking off profits from YOP schemes: 'The local authorities could therefore be proud of making a profitable response to need, the colleges had proved to be business-like, and even the YOP trainee had gained something' (*ibid*).

However, the key point about staffing has been recognized by some, for example, the FEU:

> ... LEA's and colleges should (initially at least) operate some 'positive discrimination' in favour of staff involved in vocational preparation. There should be no damage to career prospects of those willing to commit themselves to what is classified as 'low-level' work. (FEU, Jan. 1981, para. 60)

The crisis in the making, however, may derive not only through declining rolls transferring from the secondary schools to FE, but also through the MSC and government's strategic objective to reform skill training. This latter could result in a smaller FE component of work than, for example, the present apprenticeship agreements permit. This is, of course, a somewhat speculative point, yet it is a possibility perceptible to FE lecturers, and such perceptions are influential on their behaviour. If adult training does not expand, or not expand in the FE sector, and YTSs not lead to increased demand for traditional FE courses (through progression), then the scale, nature and level of FE work could be both reduced and structurally reoriented toward the grade five level. Such structural change would surely cause serious dissatisfactions for FE lecturers, both in terms of their career prospects and in terms of their own perceptions of their status and role in society in general, and in the education system in particular.

The generation of YTS teachers from this 'pool' of FE lecturers is generally seen to depend on that ubiquitous instrument, staff development. However, such an instrument cannot easily overcome basic attitudes and perceptions, built up, perhaps, over a number of years.

> Twelve years or so ago, when I encountered the first example of link courses being set up between schools and colleges, there were many FE staff who were resistant to the idea. They had not become college lecturers (and the title is significant) in order to teach school children; in fact there were those who had gone into colleges in order to get away from them. Similarly, and more recently, I had the opportunity to interview many potential entrants to the profession, in a college of education, and when asked why they particularly wanted to teach in further education, many of them would reply that they were anxious to teach a subject for which they personally had special enthusiasm, to groups of students who were mature and well motivated. (FEU, Jan. 1981, *Signposts*, p. 34)

Such attitudes are not at all uncommon, and are almost inevitably going to be exacerbated by the material deprivations created by the massive stagnation of prospects replacement work of grade five level would bring to the FE sector. Anyone with experience of FE and the Burnham system will realize that changes in the salary and status structure are not likely to proceed at a rate parallel to such changes in the distribution of the levels of work available to lecturers, particularly those who are allotted YTS work, (see, for example, Saran, 1982, pp. 173–7).

The rate and scale of the one billion pound programme mooted in the *NTI* (Dec. 1981, Govt), and already engaged with for September 1982, is such that by September 1983, as many as 15 per cent full-time equivalent FE lecturers could be involved in YTS work. This is a figure very crudely approximated from the effect of YTS on Avon LEA, where the installation of YTS is substantially advanced, and staffing implications reasonably assessable. While some YTS teachers will be specially recruited, probably on a short-term contract basis, the larger proportion will derive from the present establishment of FE lecturers. A proportion of these could be completely transferred to YTS work (whole timetables), but many will find their timetables restructured, particularly as the departmental 'servicing' mode of many FE college organizations will provide the framework in which YTS courses are mounted. With this in mind, it can be appreciated that the number of lecturers affected in some degree by YTS courses could be quite large, perhaps as many as 25 per cent. Of course, not all will have an effective timetable detriment in terms of level of work.

The main point is the general one that involvement with the 'new curriculum' is not likely to be confined to one college department or section, but to have a widespread impact. This means the 'new curriculum' in the further education sector is unlikely to be serviced by a small group of teachers highly motivated and purpose trained. The manpower input to the 'new curriculum' could be significantly diffuse in this respect. Consequently, it would be somewhat naive to suppose trainees will meet, and be taught and guided by, a coherent teacher group comprised of trained and well motivated teachers. This is not to suggest that trainees will meet disaffection on a large scale, but rather to indicate that teacher attitudes toward them (and YTS) may be ambivalent to varying degrees, if not necessarily overtly antipathetic. Essentially, the inherent need for committed and highly motivated teachers to teach the 'new curriculum' to mixed ability and possibly poorly motivated and significantly disaffected trainees may not be particularly well met. Perhaps such a view is overpessimistic, but it does need to be recognized that bland and benign 'sky-lab' assumptions about the 'human interface' in the 'new curriculum', to do with trainees and teachers' motivations, may prove to be overoptimistic. The development of trainee motivating progression, stimulated by teachers, may not, therefore, be easily achieved at the human level.

It is true, of course, that the use of a substantial number of part-time staff led by a few full-timers is a tempting organizational format for colleges. The weakness of this YOP approach is its lack of integration with overall college facilities and resources, its potential for second-class status and hiding away 'problems' in temporary annexes. In addition, there is little doubt that substantial use of part-timers leads to administrative incoherence and breakdown in curriculum organizations highly dependent on substantial administrative input. Dilution of professional and experience qualifications is also an ingredient in the overuse of part-time staff. It is not impossible to assemble an effective and well motivated teaching group on this basis, and such claims have been made by some colleges and authorities of long commitment to pre-vocational preparation. However, this is unlikely to prove the general rule, particularly in the inevitable context of under-resourcing. The choice is between recruiting a special purpose unit of teachers led by full-time staff and connected to the 'real' college through a head of department or vice-principal, or generating a grouping of teachers within the 'real' college supplemented by part-timers and short-term contract staff. Both approaches have intrinsic tendencies toward in-coherence for different reasons. In general, YTS 'new curriculum' organizations are likely to be characterised by ambiguities, confusion and poor overall direction. Organization members, especially trainees and teachers, will be plagued by uncertainties about the benefits of belonging to their organizations.

That this is an exceedingly complex matter put simply here cannot be and is not denied. The central importance of progression, as synonymous with advancement, to the motivation of trainees bears further explication, beyond the general conclusion above, that the 'new curriculum' may provide for the intersection of both poorly motivated trainees and teachers. There is, of course, a considerable body of research into human motivation which it would not be reasonable or useful to review here. Handy (1976), among others, provides a convenient collative review of such theories in Chapter 1 of his book. In any case, much of the work done relates to human motivation in work organizations. Nevertheless, certain features of current thinking on human motivation in work organizations do illuminate the matter of trainee motivation and progression in curriculum organizations.

For example, the 'Two Factor Theory' of Herzberg *et al.* (1959) indicates, in spite of criticism of his research base for the theory, that advancement (as a prospect for the individual) is an important motivator. Herzberg's theory predicts that some 'factors' dissatisfy, while others satisfy, and that a lack of dissatisfaction does not in itself cause an individual to work hard. He argued that the factors are actually of two kinds: hygiene and motivators. Hygiene factors are to do with organizational behaviours which enable people not to feel dissatisfied, such as reasonable pay, good supervisor behaviour, reasonable job security. Motivators are organizational behaviours which create satisfaction for individuals, such as recognition of achievement, interest in the work itself, prospects of advancement. Trainees dissatisfied with the hygiene factors in their curriculum organizations, such as disliking staff, may well absent themselves, or actually leave, or become psychologically absent. Trainees satisfied with motivators in their curriculum organization, such as getting recognition of achievement through membership, may well work extremely hard. Curriculum organizations which dissatisfy in Herzberg's sense, while at the same time satisfy on the motivator factors side, would be characterized by high turnover of some members, or high absenteeism, while succeeding in highly motivating other members. A combination of effective hygiene and motivator factors would produce hard working trainees and little turnover or absence, according to Herzberg.

Usefully associated with this theory is another known as expectancy theory (originally formulated by Tolman and Lewin in the 1930s, and recently applied to behaviour in organizations by, for example, Vroom, 1964, and Porter and Lawler, 1968). In very simple terms, it can be argued that trainee's perception of his prospects for advancement (progression) through membership of a 'new curriculum' organization, that is, his *expectations*, will substantially affect his motivation to work hard. This seems an obvious conclusion, which requires only common sense and not the luxury of theories to make reasonable. However, consideration of motivation theories reveals both the potential importance and the complexity of the progression/advancement factor in the 'new curriculum'. The award of a 'pass' profile certificate could mean little in terms of trainee motivation if it is perceived to have little instrumental value in getting a job and/or further education. This is to assume that trainees will indeed value such 'advancement'. It is possible that the acquisition of a high social status certificate would be enough in itself for some trainees, acting perhaps as a public symbol of success. This could effectively act as a motivator, providing YTS certificates acquire social status of public significance and recognition. The key problem in the analysis of trainee motivation is the problem of individual differences, which has, in any case, dogged the assembly of motivation theories into one coherent whole, namely a general theory of human motivation. In spite of the lack of a general theory, the concept of an individual motivational calculus set in the conceptual framework of what is known as the psychological contract, does provide a moderately efficacious tool with which to extend the analysis of trainee motivation in relation to progression.

The concept of the psychological contract has been variously explored. The point of departure taken here is that of Schein (1970), who treats the contract in terms of organizational psychology. Essentially, three kinds of psychological contract are identified: alienative, calculative and moral. These subsist in organizations. Organizations can be classed in terms of the type of power or authority used in them. Etzioni's (1961) typology indicates four types: coercive, utilitarian, normative, and mixed. There is an important sense, argued in Chapter 1, in which a curriculum is an organization, and the 'new curriculum' is treated in this way. Indeed, because it is not subject structured, that is, a collection code curriculum (Bernstein, 1971), but integrated code, trainees could more easily experience the 'new curriculum' in holistic terms. In this sense it would, in many respects, behave as an organization in the experience of trainees. Consequently, by typing 'new curriculum' organizations in Etzioni's (1961) terms, the kind of trainee involvement can be tentatively predicted.

Table 1 provides a summary in matrix form of the possible combinations of relations between organizational type and kind of trainee involvement. From Table 1 it can be seen that if trainee experience of the organization, that is, the 'new curriculum', is that of being coerced, then his involvement is likely to be characterized by alienation. The supplementary benefits effect, discussed earlier in

Table 1.   Possible Combinations of Relations between Organizational Type and Kind of Trainee Involvement

Kind of individual involvement	Organizational power/authority type			
	Coercive	Utilitarian	Normative	Mixed
Alienative	√			
Calculative		√		↕
Moral			√	↕

Source: Based on Etzioni (1961).

relation to the government's initial NTI proposal, was an obvious form of coercion and likely to be seen as such by trainees. It could be argued, too, that the pass-fail aspect of the 'new curriculum' insensitively handled could be seen as coercive. Such perception could be induced through the recording/assessment process in the 'new curriculum' when related, as it is, through the teachers themselves to the pass-fail decision. The added dimension of public profiles in the affective domain could exacerbate perception in this vein. There is, then, a potentially coercive authority/power structure in the management and administration of 'new curriculum' organizations, based directly in the teachers themselves, and not in the usual fashion with an external authority. Because, too, some trainees may feel they have 'no choice' but to sign on for a YTS course, there is a significant general prospect of them forming an alienative relationship with the 'new curriculum'.

Such alienation could be reduced or diverted if trainees could be persuaded that their organization (the 'new curriculum') has utility for them. And this is where progression is crucial. Of course, the first utility could simply be related to the provision of an allowance, which does not now have a coercive element to it in relation to supplementary benefits. However, in Herzbergian terms (1959), the allowance would be a hygiene factor, and not a motivator; trainees would be induced to remain in their courses, but not necessarily to put in motivated effort. In terms, too, of the 'Hierarchy of Needs Theory' and the Principle of Prepotence, first advanced by Abraham Maslow (1954), this would satisfy lower order needs for survival and security, releasing trainees from such predomination of their motives. However, the 'dole' and supplementary benefits would, in any case, have the same effect in this respect. Progression/advancement would therefore provide utility for trainees not predominated by Maslovian survival needs, while providing motivation in Herzbergian terms. Trainees are likely to be dominated by social, self-esteem (ego), and perhaps self-actualization needs, in Maslovian terms, when the utility of progression/advancement would be potentially significant to their satisfaction. Acquisition of public social status from a YTS profile certificate is unlikely because the intrinsic worth of certificates in this respect is almost certain to be of a low order. Consequently, social or self-esteem needs are unlikely to be satisfied simply through the acquisition of a certificate.

From this it can be appreciated that trainees would be involved in 'new curriculum' organizations in respect of their utility, which Etzioni's typology (Table 1) predicts as one of calculative relation. For such a relationship to be sustained, and not lapse into the alienative, trainees must be able to reasonably calculate that the 'new curriculum' does in fact hold utility for them. Such utility depends entirely on their perception of there being first a relation between their performance in the 'new curriculum' and its outcomes for them; and, second, that they value its outcomes, or, at least, one of them.

Such a view of trainee motivation significantly involves the 'expectancy-instrumental theory' of motivation, propounded by, for example, Porter and Lawler (1968) and reviewed by Mitchell and Biglan (1971). Allowing for individual differences as illustrated, for example, by McClelland's (1953) theory of 'achievement motive', trainees might be persuaded to early establish an expectation of advancement which they value, with the 'new curriculum' being the instrument by which they achieve their expectation. Providing the 'instrumentality' of the 'new curriculum' seems to them an effective one in this respect, they may be motivated to put high effort into the course. Such effort would derive in a calculative relationship and depend on trainees valuing at least one of the hierarchy of possible outcomes, and believing there is a relationship between their level of effort and getting what they value.

It is possible that normative pressures could be significant to the running of YTS courses. This would give high salience to views such as the traditional 'education' is a good thing, 'there's nothing like training, nothing like getting a trade', 'society is doing its best by you, spending millions', etc. Should the 'new curriculum' depend on such normative authority, then trainees would, after Etzioni (1961), be involved on a moral basis. They would do the course, because it was the *right* thing to do, because training and education are intrinsically good things.

Certainly, such normative pressures are generated by substantial social opinion, perhaps even now resurging after a period of decline. Trainees would simply put high effort into the 'new curriculum' because they felt morally obliged to do so. Whether teachers should rely on trainees having such a moral relation to the 'new curriculum' is somewhat dubious. Schein's (1970) assessment can be usefully quoted at length here, although about university students.

> One way of looking at what is happening on many university campuses is that students are shifting the basis of their involvement from *moral* (being in college because they value education for its own sake) or *calculative* (being in college because education pays off in better jobs and better future income) toward *alienative* (being in college only because of pressure to be there and finding educational offerings irrelevant, hypocritical, or degrading). In other words, the traditional normative authority

of the professor based on this scholarly expertise in a given area of inquiry can function only so long as students accept this expertise as relevant to their own values and goals. Once they define the professor's expertise as irrelevant, the professor no longer has any rational authority. He must then rely on utilitarian authority (hope that students will see the need of an education for their own future economic well-being) or coercive authority (threaten to flunk students who are disrespectful or fail to do their work). Much of the anger of the student and the anxiety of the professor is due to the breakdown of the psychological contract between them. (Schein, 1970, pp. 54–5)

The psychological contract of YTS trainees with their 'new curriculum' organization is most unlikely to take the form of an intrinsic valuing of membership for its own sake. It would not be reasonable to predict a broad moral involvement and relation between trainee and the 'new curriculum'. Consequently, YTS teachers may easily find themselves in the predicament of Schein's professor: stressing the instrumental value of the course to trainees' for their 'advancement' in life, and hinting at teachers' power to 'flunk' trainees who do not conform in behaviour and/or work hard at the 'new curriculum'. For this 'strategy' of motivation to work trainees must generally have a calculative involvement with the 'new curriculum'. Table 1 suggests, in effect, that the 'new curriculum' should be utilitarian, in terms of its authority type, to match such calculative trainee involvement. Consequently, progression/advancement will provide the main instrument of its utility; but only providing trainees perceive the progressions as related to their effort, while at the same time actually valuing (wanting) such. In these terms a framework for the motivational calculus of trainees can be devised using Handy's (1976) model (his Chapter 2). Figure 12 provides a diagrammatic illustration of a model of trainees' motivational calculus. Nevertheless, it cannot be overlooked that many trainees will assuredly start out their involvement with the 'new curriculum' on the borderline of a calculative and alienative relation to it, the 'new curriculum' behaving for them ambivalently between coercive and utilitarian.

Handy's model does not take into account certain importance variables, not least of which is that of antecedent attitudes (that reward/result valuation, perceived probability and role perception are crucial antecedents to the calculus) after Lawler and Porter (1976, pp. 122–42). This is to say, in simple terms, that individual differences between trainees, together with the attitudes, opinions, and perceptions which they have *before* going to a YTS, will be important influences on

Figure 12. Diagrammatic Illustration of YTS Trainees' Motivational Calculus

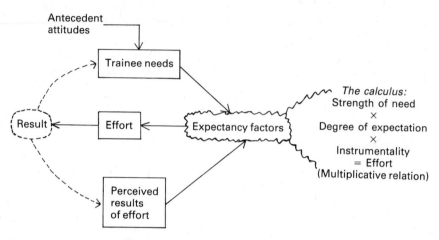

Source: Based on Handy (1976), Chapter 2.

their behaviour in the YTS, irrespective of what they experience during its process. Figure 12 does not fully express or account for this, but it still provides an instrument of analysis useful for the broad assessment of *general* trainee behaviour in 'new curriculum' organizations.

From Herzberg (1959) it can be seen that the need for achievement correlates with Maslow's (1954) higher order needs. In these terms, a trainee's need for achievement is a motivator of effort, but this is providing a trainee can have some reasonable (to him) expectation of succeeding (after McClelland, 1953), and also a belief that his effort can in fact lead to the achievement (after Porter and Lawler, 1968). Achievement can be treated in psychological Maslovian terms, as an intrinsic success rewarded or affirmed by applause sourced internally by YTS 'new curriculum' organizations, for example, teachers awarding good marks, or praising. Alternatively, or in addition, it can be treated in the utilitarian terms of extrinsic success, externally sourced by awarding a trainee valued progression, such as a job, a 'real' course. Psychological intrinsic rewarding would depend for success in motivating trainees on whether this was socially valued, in the sense of enabling or advancing trainees' social cohesion or status in a group, in other words, rewarding their need to belong. This marginal higher order Maslovian need could, of course, be satisfied in contrary ways not conducive to the objects of teachers and other 'owners' of 'new curriculum' organizations. Group esteem could, for example, accrue to the biggest nuisance. Higher order needs of esteem and self–actualization may offer some scope for the management of intrinsic rewards, internally sourced. It could be a serious error to suppose that higher order needs must be to do with cognitive achievements of specially high order.

Broadly, then, and although the calculus is different for each individual, there are three separate elements involved: the strength (or salience) of the need; the expectancy that effort will lead to a particular result; and the instrumentality of that result reducing the need. Handy's example is simple but effective.

> . . . a man who has a high need for power if given a task to do and promised promotion at the end of it will expend energy on the task to the degree that he believes: that good performance will lead to promotion (expectance); that promotion will satisfy his power needs (instrumentality).
>
> If either of these conditions do not apply he will not expend energy over and above that needed to keep him employed (assuming that his need for security is operating). (Handy, 1976, p. 36)

Handy goes on to argue that the relation between strength of need, expectancy and instrumentality is *multiplicative* (see Figure 12). This means that if one element is zero then the whole sum is zero, resulting in no effort.

It is not unreasonable to assume that trainees' basic Maslovian needs will be catered for by the training allowance, and generally in any case because of their probable residence in the parental home. However, their higher order needs are very much to be associated with their prospects in the world of work. The fact that they become members of a YTS 'new curriculum' organization suggests, at the least, they have not found work they wish to do, and that they desire the training allowance. It is upon what purpose they see their YTS serving that the operation of the motivational calculus depends. Quite clearly if it is limited to satisfying the 'basic need' for a training allowance, trainees simply have to reside in the scheme, and this they can do without effort. Indeed, coercive 'carrot and stick' methods to incite effort by expelling non-effort making trainees from their YTS (that is, from the allowance) would produce no effect whatsoever, except perhaps to realign (or affirm) a calculative relation to an alienated relation for those who remain.

Some trainees may simply have no purpose, or no conscious,

articulated purpose, in 'life'. However, it would be an unreasonable presumption to generally suppose that trainees have no higher order needs. Consequently, trainees could be generally encouraged to see their YTS as an instrument for advancement, an instrument which will permit them to 'achieve' a job, to achieve one of the possible outcomes of the 'new curriculum' they value. The guidance and counselling process provides opportunity to persuade trainees that effort on their part will be instrumental in achieving an 'achievement' outcome, while also, at the same time, schooling them in the merits and demerits of the outcomes that are possible, including the presumption of a correlation between the simple unemployment outcome and a poor (that is, fail) profile certificate.

However, teachers would be ill advised to promise trainees that hard work will lead to a 'good' certificate, and that a good certificate will lead to a job. Such guarantee is beyond what is in the power of MSC to grant, let alone teachers. But, YTS teachers, operating within FE as the provider organization (LEA/college), may well be able to indicate that further training or entry into a 'real' further education course, although without allowances, would be possible, and would be based on trainees' certificates. It can be seen immediately that the question of further support through allowances is central to this aspect of progression. Without a change of government such support is likely to be limited and highly selective. Nevertheless, something can be offered, flawed though it is by the allowance problem, which could have instrumentality for trainees. The tendency for substantial YTS provision to be generated by employers' Managing Agencies is significant. The use of the additionality rules (two normal young entrants yields an allowance for five trainees if the employer takes five instead of two) enables employers to very usefully expand the catchment for selecting recruits for their training schemes, as mentioned in Chapter 3. The YTS can be, and in some pilot schemes was used, to improve the recruitment processes of companies at little or no cost. Trainees in direct employer schemes have therefore a material prospect of being subsequently recruited by the company on the basis of their individual YTS performances. Conversely, of course, others will *fail* to get an offer of employment, although, perhaps, 'passing' the course.

There are ways, therefore, in which a psychological contract of calculative/utilitarian relation could be constructed, on the progression/advancement basis, between trainees and the 'new curriculum'. What is clear, though, is that such contracts are very susceptible to breakdown through uncertainties, confusions and ambiguities about outcomes.

This is likely to be compounded by the prospect and possibility that trainees will perceive the 'new curriculum' as another 'con', that high effort on their part will not be instrumental in determining a needed outcome. This is to argue that the progression/advancement element in the 'new curriculum' based in the assessment and certification process is likely to prove a crucial determinant of trainee investment of motivated effort. It is to observe, too, that the process of progression/advancement in the 'new curriculum' is certainly problematic and perhaps that it is fatally flawed.

However, two kinds or types of 'new curriculum' organizations may evolve under the MSC (YTS) aegis: an *education progression* model; and a *job-recruitment progression* model. In the former the 'school' or college off-the-job training element of the 'new curriculum' organization would be dominant, perhaps reaching the maximum of twenty-six weeks. This model could easily evolve under LEA Managing Agencies. YTS courses of this kind could be geared to inducing trainee progression to higher courses, vocational and 'relevant' education. Whether non-vocational education could ever be regarded as relevant in this respect is doubtful in practice, although by no means theoretically ruled out. In the latter, work experience would be dominant, with minimum off-the-job training of thirteen weeks. This model could easily evolve under employer-based Managing Agencies which buy in or provide minimum off-the-job training. The job-recruitment progression model may induce (what many young people want) increasingly job-specific training of direct use to those who succeed in the related recruiting process of the employer. Those not chosen for the jobs or apprenticeships that do exist at the end of their particular 'new curriculum' organizations, while failing in that respect, could still get a 'pass' profile. This kind of organization would be characterized by the material prospect of a job-progression seemingly related to individual performance in their 'new curriculum' organization. Short-time horizon trainees might seem most suited to such organizations, especially if their achievement motive is simple in Maslovian terms. It would be easy to develop such analysis in a simplistic way and reach misleading conclusions. However, at this stage it is sufficient to point out that the two kinds of 'new curriculum' organizations are likely to behave in importantly different ways. This could have significant implications in respect of the effective management of the different kinds of 'new curriculum' organizations. It is possible that sufficient difference between the two models may become established such that they could be regarded as two distinct curricula.

There is, then, little doubt that any insensitivity on the part of teachers in handling this more complex aspect of the 'new curriculum' could have an apparently disproportionate dis-motivational effect on trainees, and easily cause them to align in an alienative relation. That trainees should put high effort into the 'new curriculum' is assumed to be intrinsically desirable, and extrinsically to improve their prospects in life, that is, because of effort they will for the larger part progress. The 'chicken and egg' aspect of this is clear, if complex. Trainees in calculative relation to the 'new curriculum' will put high effort into it so far as they believe it an efficacious instrument for their progress/advancement. This assumes trainees will be subject to predominantly higher order Maslovian needs, among which achievement is a related Herzbergian motivator, along with the work itself, a sense of responsibility, recognition and growth. Trainees disaffected with the reality (or perception) of the outcomes of the 'new curriculum' will 'switch off' and 'coast'.

Broadly, then, *progression* is taken to be a central, fundamental, key determinant of trainee motivation, irrespective of whether teachers could construct other satisfiers of trainee needs. This latter 'technique' could be most effective with what Handy (1976) calls 'short horizon' trainees. In other words, individuals whose motivational calculus has a short time span.

> Small children appear to make almost instinctive calculations aimed at almost immediate results. As they grow up the calculus seems to become more conscious, and often as a result more complicated, and their time-span for pay-off rather longer. (Handy, 1976, p. 37)

Trainees, it should not be forgotten, are young adults, if largely of assumed low attainment and/or ability. Perhaps, with such a long history of poor 'achievement', minimal recognition, and so on, such young adults could locate value within the fifty-two-week time-horizon of the 'new curriculum', if sensitively managed by teachers. Nevertheless, many are likely to be in the grip of a time-horizon set firmly in the material framework of the course being or not being a means of getting a job they value.

Referring back to the range of possible substantive outcomes for trainees in the 'new curriculum', it can be seen that a job with prospects cannot be guaranteed even for those with exceptionally good (pass) profile certificates. This is particularly true of the education progression model, and less true of the job-recruitment progression model when effective competitive performance may clearly result in being recruited. It is noteworthy that employers' 'normal' recruits would be mixed with YTS trainees, who would presumably not normally have been recruited into first-year training schemes. How such competition will work out in practice may, of course, be different to the easy prediction that 'ordinary' trainees will not compete successfully with 'normal' first-year trainees. However, in the education progression model further training and education could be, if (unlike jobs) suitable places were provided on demand. Apart from the problem of continuing or extending personal trainee allowances, this would involve interfacing a range of vocational courses provided in a locality. It would involve, too, orienting the education progression model to individual preparation for further education in the context of flexible entrance to existing provision. This would require a major curricular review of further education itself. But curriculum in further education is a subject of immense proportion:

> The historical foundation of further education courses is response to a perceived need; curricular study as a whole has never yet been taken forward, and even the Further Education Curriculum Review and Development Unit has preferred to investigate areas where needs require fulfilling. (NATFHE, 1980, p. 449).

However, the dynamic of the further education service is 'response to perceived need'. Whether need is perceived in market or moral terms, response is the order of the day.

It is conceivable, therefore, that the 'new curriculum' could well provide a genuine basis for the formation of a much simplified routing for young people to further education and employment. The present plethora of provision has been more than adequately criticized over the last few years, as indicated in Chapter 3. With the pressure of YTS there could be a greater possibility of a general and coherent recognition of the 'new curriculum' being a general instrument for pre-vocational preparation significant to established and developing FE curricula. As already discussed above, the FEU (Dec. 1981) identified a strategic link between pre-vocational preparation and such curricula in terms of the level 1, level 2 distinction. That this is a crucial link was developed in Chapter 3 with the argument that the 'new curriculum' is preventative of trainees progressing to HE defined curricula. Consequently, the full range of FE provision in this respect is irrelevant to a concept (and practice) of progression which could be reasonably associated with the 'new curriculum'. This leaves, using FEU (Jan. 1981) terms (c.f. Figure 7, 8 and 9 above), curricula defined by claimed job demands.

TEC and BEC have, since 1973 and 1974 respectively, come to dominate FE curricula and their certification. The City and Guilds of London Institute (CGLI) has progressively taken over the administration of the Joint Committee courses, but on behalf of TEC, in line with the recommendations of the Haslegrave Committee (1969). Consequently, CGLI technician courses and Joint Committee courses have effectively merged under the TEC validation process, leaving craft (high job specific) courses under CGLI. A parallel process has occurred in the business education field, under BEC. Consequently, non-employment progression reduces to the 'new curriculum' serving for TEC and BEC level 1 courses, if this can be agreed, or entry into craft training among the range of CGLI, RSA and comparable courses which can be locally provided. Figure 13 illustrates non-employment progression for YTS trainees.

Through the basic skills structure of the education progression model of the YTS 'new curriculum', trainees may be able to progress to level 2 programmes. Trainees should acquire basic skills through motivated effort while members of a 'new curriculum' organization. Common core, vocational sampling and occupational skills comprise basic skills and are intended to provide the foundation for progression to level 2 programmes. Figure 13 shows the present relationship

Figure 13. Non-Employment Progression for YTS Trainees

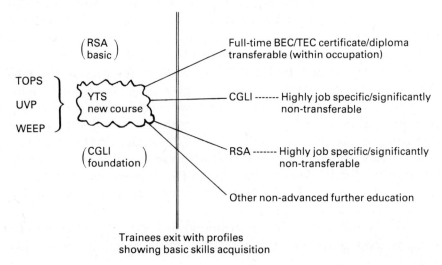

between the 'new curriculum' and FE provision. It can be seen that the FEU case for developing the Hargreaves Committee (June 1981) process-in-common skills as a way of inducing significant transferability of skills into what follows for YTS trainees is crucial. Nevertheless, even these are narrowly and not necessarily widely transferable. The present range of progression is inadequately related to the ideal of a 'new curriculum', and much needs to be done to correlate the FEU ideal type with present FE curricula. This means developing and changing both entry requirements and the capacity of FE curricula to sustain skill ownership and transferability in the face of the problematic contradiction of their inherent aim, which is to prepare individuals to do jobs. The YTS 'new curriculum' could indeed prepare trainees for progression to further education on a foundation of basic skills. It could regularize trainees' experience such that many could 'succeed' in this. Their basic skills would be owned by them and be significantly transferable and not simply job-specific, perhaps at the least being job-cluster-specific, involving process-in-common skills.

However, this, in the education progression model, leads to existing FE curricula which are largely either technician level or craft level. Technician level curricula do provide skill transferability, within occupations at least. However, craft level curricula are, at present, no more than job-cluster-specific, if not simply job-specific. Obviously, the end object of further vocational education is to prepare students for work in particular occupations, and ultimately for particular jobs. It should not be assumed that local 'techs' do not continue to reverberate to the cry for *relevance* from employers and students alike. There is surely a significant and problematic dilemma in this. Added to which, the education progression model of the 'new curriculum' could succeed (too well) in bringing on bottom half youngsters, feeding them into further education, qualification and thence to *their* jobs?

Such progression could be established using the internal skills development structure of occupational families in the 'new curriculum'. Selection for the 'advanced' progression to level 2 TEC or BEC courses could be made using the profile certification process to determine which trainees would be likely to benefit from technician level courses. Manual and office/clerical skills, among those trainees not selected for technician level courses, would provide a base for specific job training in the CGLI/RSA framework. The questionable feature of this latter progression is that it assumes certain short-term future demands in the national and local labour market. Because the CGLI/RSA framework of training is still essentially job-specific, trainee progression through this form of training will establish, or fix, trainees with substantially non or narrowly transferable skills. Conversely, those trainees progressing to TEC/BEC curricula are less liable to acquire such highly job-specific skills, although their skills will, of course, be *occupationally* oriented.

In general, then, progression to further training within the FE sector could simply defer unemployment especially for those trainees progressing through the CGLI/RSA framework, unless demand recovers, and if it recovers, does not reveal a significant residuum of structural unemployment. It will be remembered that the central conceptual feature of developing a curriculum which substantially aimed to provide trainees with transferable skills was to ensure flexibility in the labour market generally, so that structurally *changing* demands could be met. It can, and perhaps should, be argued that such a sophisticated aim would in any case fall between the two stools of trainee capability, on the one side, and a substantial overestimation of the rate of structural change, on the other. In other words, trainees with generalized, but transferable skills, would in any case need to do a job, and would subsequently need retraining to do another at some later stage of their lives: transferability of skills will not substitute for retraining, and 'low ability' trainees cannot be expected to acquire the extensive self-learning capacities associated with the effects of advanced further education (AFE) and higher education (HE) curricula.

The 'new curriculum' does provide trainees with scope for career decision in its latter stages. Indeed, trainees are fundamentally obliged to 'experience' and to learn skills associated with a particular occupational family following the 'sampling' process. Presumably, trainees will be sufficiently enthralled by such experience and skills acquisition that they will be motivated to continue in further education, in order to proceed through a specialized curriculum associated with that family. However, in terms of trainees' motivational calculus, progression to occupationally specific training may involve a calculation that a job must eventually be materially related to their efforts in acquiring such skills. Guarantees on that front remain elusive, of course. Nevertheless, the CGLI/RSA framework can provide a material outcome for some selected trainees, which amounts to advancement. In this trainees are making the minimum advance against the alternative of further or new unemployment. The best trainees can expect, or should be led to expect, is advancement to the technician level provided by TEC/BEC curricula. This distinction between trainees would depend on their performance in the 'new curriculum', which would be recorded in their profile certificates. Consequently, selection between TEC/BEC progression and CGLI/RSA progression would depend on the profile certification process.

It takes little perspective to appreciate a certain sense of redundancy about this aspect of progression through the 'new curriculum'. This is to say that, apart from trainee allowances, there are already established avenues for 16-year-olds to progress in this way. For those who succeed in the traditional CSE and GCE framework, CGLI/RSA and TEC/BEC courses are open. For those who do not, CGLI foundation and RSA basic courses could provide an equivalent route to the present range of CGLI/RSA craft courses. However, what could be established through the provision of 'new curriculum' organizations is both an improved *catchment* system and an improved *selection* system.

The education progression model of the 'new curriculum' as a catchment system operates in three main ways. It may, first of all, collect or net large numbers of 16- and 17-year-olds who would not have become involved in any form of further training in the past. Once 'netted' by a 'new curriculum' organization, and motivated in it, it is possible that many could progress to further education and training because they have acquired both common core skills and have had an opportunity to sample, before choosing, skills training in a particular occupational family. Having made an informed choice, trainees may in fact succeed in their skills acquisition and be encouraged by success (achievement) to continue in further education. As a selection system, the 'new curriculum' enables informed guidance and direction to be made available to the 'netted' 16–17-year-olds. At the same time it enables each trainee to be assessed and such assessment to be recorded and ultimately profiled, thus enabling employers and/or colleges to make selections for their own purposes.

These benefits are presently available, but in a partial and incoherent fashion. The 'new curriculum' provides a stimulus, an instrument to create coherence and wider coverage of the 16- and 17-year-old cohort leaving secondary education. It is in this respect an important instrument for the furtherance of a national manpower policy which aims, among other things, to restructure the skills dimensions of the working population. In this respect the most serious problem is to reduce the size of the unskilled pool. As discussed in Chapter 2, this is a somewhat simplistic notion, which suffers from the continuing unreliability and imprecision of predictions about future manpower requirements. Nevertheless, even such basic direction is, perhaps, better than none at all.

It has been argued in this chapter that progression is important, perhaps vitally so, both to manpower policy and to the successful motivation of individual trainees entering the 'new curriculum'. The success of the 'new curriculum' as a manpower policy instrument is interdependent with its success in effectively motivating young leavers to participate with high effort. Progression is necessary to trainee motivation in this latter respect, but is also necessary to the replacement of training and education no longer provided through employment. The present concept of progression in these respects was found to be seriously flawed. In addition, it was argued that the 'new curriculum' would be effectively preventative of progression in the upper range of a tentative hierarchy of outcomes. Associated with this was the 'intellectual apartheid' effect. The 'new curriculum', in its present form and context, reinforces the present structure of education curricula, maintaining such apartheid. Division of interest between the MSC and DES/LEAs leaves serious ambiguity about the future status of the profile certification involved in the 'new curriculum', together with a doubtful relationship between it and the proposed secondary/tertiary 17+ pre-vocational leaving certificate. However, the 'new curriculum' is significantly a catchment system for young people considerably neglected in the past. It is also a selection system, using its certification process to 're-trawl', as it were, for fish not caught by the somewhat tattered nets of the old fleet of examinations.

Not forgetting (who could):

> The great god Mediocrity is always willing to look after his own. If you are not good enough for university and have to put up with a college of education, perhaps a B.Ed. may come your way, or you may find a technical college to give you a CNAA degree – and, failing all this, there will soon be the Open University. I still prefer Oxford and Cambridge, no matter how exotic the combination of the alphabet that is offered. Or again, if GCE is beyond you, CSE will oblige. They are 'reasonable'; they pass about ninety-five per cent of their entry ... But then they make up their own syllabuses as well. Welcoming the proposals from which this beautiful baby emerged, two writers on education claimed that 'a *qualifying* examination should be set at a standard at which about four-fifths of the candidates will qualify' ... Their cup's full and running over, but I am not sure that many outside bodies or employers are keen to drink of it. (Pollard, undated, p. 72)

It might be supposed, perhaps, that even small beer needs labelling; some bodies presumably imbibe less than champagne. Should not small beer, in any case, be up to certain standards in a competitive consumer market? Small beer ought to be mechanically literate, computationally numerate and politically stable and produced by 'new curriculum' organizations. The dangers of such simplicities are well known to babies in bathwaters.

5   Conclusions

The major input into social organizations consists of people.
The economist or the culturologist may concentrate on inputs
of resources, raw materials, technology. To the extent that
human factors are recognized, they are assumed to be constants
in the total equation and are neglected. At the practical level,
however, as well as for a more precise theoretical accounting,
we need to cope with such organizational realities as the
attracting of people into organizations, holding them within the
system, insuring reliable role performance, and in addition
stimulating actions which are generally facilitative of organizational accomplishment. The material and psychic returns to
organizational members thus constitute major determinants,
not only of the level of effectiveness of organizational function-
ing, but of the very existence of the organization.

Katz, 1964, p. 131

A tentative starting point for a new definition of curriculum has
evolved through the process of attempting to use the concept, outlined
in Chapter 1, of curriculum as organization (s). A definition could go
something like this:

Curriculum means a distinct kind, type or category of organizational activity which regularizes the experience of learner
members for educational or training purposes, the effects of
which *could* be measured against their individual behaviours
entering or during and/or exiting from a curriculum organization.

A curriculum can be comprised of one, few or many individual curriculum organizations. When it is comprised of more than one such organization the degree of organizational commonality or similarity between them establishes their differentiation into distinct types, and this typification nominates distinct curricula.

Commonality is to do with organizational similarities between compositions, structure, management and purposes generating similar individual and organizational behaviours.

Individual curriculum organizations exist when learners (people in learner roles who are members of a curriculum organization) are spatially and temporally congregated and share a common structuring or regularization of their experience for explicit or implicit education or training purposes and are subject in common to any 'unconscious' (accidental) purpose of the organization.

At this point there is considerable pressure to expand in general on the contentions and implications of the above sketch. There is an obvious necessity, for example, to argue the distinction between treating curriculum organizations, as defined here, as organizations or as social groups, However, such expansion must needs be reserved for another place. In the meantime, the definition serves to improve the focus of discussion and conclusions in this chapter, if in a somewhat rough and ready way.

It seems certain that during the next few years 'new curriculum' organizations will proliferate in the English education system and on its periphery in employing organizations. The incentive for their proliferation has come from, and will continue to come from, the MSC. Government control of MSC funding will ensure political direction to the scale, location, resourcing and quality of 'new curriculum' organizations. Technocratic influence will remain substantial and reflect the latest state of the art of labour market prediction, together with institutionalized expert opinion on vocational preparation. The phenomena of 'new curriculum' organizations, although incipient, are not likely to prove mere ephemera. The previous chapters have attempted to predict their appearance and behaviour. What follows is an attempt to draw the main ideas together.

Chapter 2 established a broad context for the emergence of 'new curriculum' organizations, with particular emphasis on labour market and manpower policy analysis. From this it was concluded that an effective national manpower training policy for young people would necessarily be dependent on rapid response to the needs of the labour market because prediction was only reliable in the very short term. In addition, youth unemployment was related to the problem of an outer-outer labour market in which many bottom half youngsters could become permanently trapped. Youth unemployment in general was predicted to remain at seriously high levels over the next few years, as an aspect of continuing general demand-deficiency. Structural unemployment was argued to be a significant underlying feature of continuing high levels of unemployment. The present incapacity of manpower analysis to predict what skills, where and when they would be needed beyond the very short term is likely to continue. Consequently, an upsurge in general demand for labour cannot be adequately differentiated into *specific* future jobs by quantity and location. Training for specific job skills was, in this respect, made problematic. The only general expectation of some credibility is that an upsurge in general demand would reveal a structural shift in the character of the demand, and that this would create severe frictional unemployment unless the skills structure of the unemployed pool (or reserve) of labour in the economy could be generally upgraded in advance. Upgrading of skills is thought necessary because the historic decline in demand for traditional craft skills is expected to continue, and be reflected even more significantly when (if) general demand increases. In addition, the demand for unskilled and semi-skilled labour is not expected to be sufficient to absorb or mop up large numbers of untrained, unqualified youngsters as in the past. Irrespective, then, of the general economic question of whether demand-deficiency will decline, the specific question of preparing against severe frictional and continuing involuntary unemployment relates to the political imperative of 'doing something' about youth unemployment.

'Something' is being done under the general national manpower training policy enunciated by the MSC and government in terms of a New Training Initiative. The NTI is aimed broadly to prepare the working population in general for structural shift in demand, and in particular at unemployed adults and young people in this respect. Out of this, the particular policy instrument of the MSC Youth Training Scheme emerged. Its purpose is to prepare young people of low school attainment for work, and to reduce the number counted as unemployed. It is related to, and an arm of, a general strategy for preparing against severe frictional unemployment in the case of future demand being structurally shifted. It is specifically concerned to prevent increasing disadvantage to low attainment, unskilled and inexperienced minimum age school leavers.

It is in this general context and manpower policy perspective that 'new curriculum' YTS organizations have been induced to proliferate by the MSC. Their purpose is related mainly to the needs of a putative national economy and these are conflated with individual needs for education and training. It is presumed that membership of YTS 'new curriculum' organizations will coincidentally satisfy the needs and aspirations of the individual low attainment youngster, the needs of a putative future economy and the immediate political imperative, described by one writer as 'moral panic' (Mungham, 1982), to do something about youth unemployment.

Some basic features of 'new curriculum' organizations were assembled in Chapter 3. From these, and the arguments in Chapter 4, several conclusions can be drawn about their likely behaviour. Before summarizing these, a distinction between practical and ideal 'new curriculum' organizations needs amplifying. Obviously, it will need a second episode of study to determine what real 'new curriculum' organizations actually do emerge and operate in society. At this stage there are various reasonable expectations about this which range from the optimistic belief that the FEU ideal model will in practice operate on a large scale, to the least optimistic belief that in practice an unsophisticated, poorly managed and somewhat reactionary training model will operate on a large scale, rubber-stamped by MSC concerned with through-put. The following general points of conclusion assume the endless reiteration of serious education and training intent by MSC and by government are seriously administered through the Area Manpower Boards and effectually applied from the centre by MSC's Youth Training Board and Advisory Group on Content and Standards. This is admittedly a large assumption, even in the longer term. The simplest analysis of the powers of the bodies illustrates the intrinsic weaknesses of controls over what happens on the ground in individual 'new curriculum' organizations. Consequently, the assumption that the *will* does exist to generate quality 'new curriculum' organizations only satisfies a necessary but not sufficient condition of effective implementation. Not least of other necessary conditions is the sufficient resourcing of an ideal model which is clearly very resource intensive.

'New curriculum' organizations will tend to require substantial, detailed administrative record keeping systems and a high degree of effective management input, both to maintain and operate these systems, and to organize complex trainee movements in an intricate timetabling framework to achieve the on and off-the-job work experience and training (education) aims of the organization. In addition, personal, careers and general formative counselling and guidance will ensure a total management, administration and teaching resource drain on a 'new curriculum' organization aspiring to the ideal model which is very substantial indeed. Add to this the prospect of bottom half leavers forming a major proportion of trainee membership of 'new curriculum' organizations with probable negative antecedent attitudes, and teacher debilitation is likely to be significant and additionally resource draining. Add to this a definite prospect of some higher ability leavers being pulled to YTS by personal allowances, and pushed by unemployment, and mixed ability teaching becomes a likely feature of teacher loading, combined with some remedial teaching requirements. Join present low funding proposals with a teacher resource pool characterized by inexperience and a disincentive career framework, and the prospects of ideal 'new curriculum' organizations emerging are not high. *If* the ideal is to be associated with quality, then the resource framework seems set to induce poor quality 'new curriculum' organizations on a large scale.

If this is the case, however, then the potential totalitarianism of ideal 'new curriculum' organizations may be obviated, by accident as it were. This is to say that the FEU ideal of formative and summative profiling leading to certification will collapse without a resource intensive administrative and professional base. Consequently, certificates will be signed, as usual, although of an unfamiliar format, but assuredly of low status and perhaps vaguely negative significance. Detailed publication will not be required of affective domain judgements based on common criteria and measures (to be somehow worked out), together with cognitive and psychomotor assessments. Intensive and extensive scrutiny of individual trainees' behaviour throughout their membership of a 'new curriculum' organization will not be needed. To achieve an objective and just profile statement of the ideal order would inevitably lead to totalitarian behaviour on the part of the organization. Such behaviour could construct an accidentally coercive authority regime in the organization, leading (after Schein, 1970) to a generally alienative relation between trainee members and the organization. Reduction of the scrutinization of trainees by teachers using a practical if less than ideal profiling system may increase the prospect of their forming a calculative relation to their 'new curriculum' organization, providing it seems to have utility for them. Such reduction would also assist teachers to form less ambiguous counselling and helping roles in the organization. Conversely, the low status of profile certificates would be confirmed by obvious lack of scope and credibility of measurement against a profusion of doubtful standards actually in place on the ground, although perhaps 'operational' in the rarefied remoteness of a 'sky-lab' committee on content and standards.

The question of the utility of 'new curriculum' organizations was argued in Chapter 4 to be fundamental to their success in motivating trainee members to expend high effort to learn. It was concluded, in general, that the emergence of effective learning (cf. working) behaviours in curriculum organizations depends importantly on the capacity of the organization to motivate its learner members, irrespective of their individual intrinsic abilities (intelligence). 'New curriculum' organizations are likely to be problematic in this respect, because trainees' perceptions of utility are likely to be highly correlated with their need for advancement and recognition. If YTS certificates turn out to be low status, their utility as instruments of recognition will be poor. Consequently, trainees' membership of 'new curriculum' organizations must have other utility to satisfy their need for advancement. Advancement was related to prospects of progression, and progression was associated with outcomes of membership of 'new curriculum' organizations. A tentative hierarchy of outcomes was identified which suggested trainees' prospects for advancement were significantly limited, and indeed membership of a 'new curriculum' organization was actually preventative of outcomes associated with individual upward socio-economic mobility. It was concluded that advancement is confined to further education and training in craft skills or level 2 further education (but without personal allowances) and/or getting a job. Both these general avenues of progression were seen to be problematic and related to the probable emergence of two kinds or models of YTS 'new curriculum' organizations.

A job-recruitment model is likely to emerge under employer-led YTS initiatives, and an education progression model in LEA-led initiatives. Job-recruitment model 'new curriculum' organizations are likely to operate with minimum thirteen weeks off-the-job training, and multiply the recruitment catchment of employing organizations by the five for two principle of the MSC's additionality rule. Trainees will compete for a limited number of *real* jobs during their YTS year in a job-recruitment model 'new curriculum' organization. Those 'passing' will get the jobs, those 'failing' will get YTS certificates. With the prospect of a 'chance at a real job', the job-recruitment model does have utility for trainees, and this could certainly ensure motivation, if somewhat coercive in the respect that the standards applicable to getting a job are not fixed but on the sliding-scale of inter-trainee competition. What happens to those who 'fail' to get jobs, and yet get 'pass' profile certificates, that is, good reports?

In the education progression model, it was argued, use of the twenty-six weeks maximum off-the-job training would be a minimum requirement to bring significant numbers of trainees toward a successful level 2 transition. Such transition would depend, at least, on institutional acceptance of YTS certificates, and on trainees being themselves persuaded such progression had utility for them, and upon the general extension of personal allowances. Those 'failing' in the job-recruitment model could use their 'pass' certificates to enter an education progression model 'new curriculum' organization. This would enable them to progress, but would depend, again, on the personal allowances link. In addition, the education progression model would need to be underwritten in terms of subsequent courses and places being available 'on demand'.

The education progression model could more easily conform to the FEU ideal, providing, of course, a sufficiency of funding were available to generate adequate space, teaching and material resources. The job-recruitment model would conform to the recruitment needs of employing organizations, and would not generally conform to the FEU ideal. However, this would be irrelevant to employers and to those trainees 'passing' into actual jobs/apprenticeships. The model could in effect replace the first year of the developing and changing apprenticeship training process. However, those 'failing' to pass into jobs or 'second'-year apprenticeships would find themselves 'locked out' of jobs elsewhere if, as seems likely, large numbers of employing organizations supply job-recruitment model 'new curriculum' organizations. Consequently, the education progression model, and its concomitants, will be needed as provision for those not placed in job-recruitment model 'new curriculum' organizations, and for those exiting from them after one year.

In paradoxically opposite respects delivery of 'quality' off-the-job training and delivery of quality relevant work experience are seriously problematic for 'new curriculum' organizations. In the education progression model the arrangement and delivery of relevant work experience is going to be extremely problematic, both in terms of finding employers willing and still able to provide places, and in terms of ensuring these are adequately related to the individual trainee.

Conversely, the job-recruitment model (using up many of the employer work experience placements) may have difficulty in delivering quality off-the-job training, perhaps finally depending on an ad hoc relationship with a local 'tech'. Youngsters' experience of work and training may suffer from, to use the vernacular, 'cock-ups', which may result in some dilution of 'quality' and cause disaffection among trainees.

Figure 14 illustrates the general relationship between the two models. It suggests neither model will generate 'new curriculum' organizations of either pure type, but each will incorporate significant features of the other. The term 'quality' is shown to be applicable to either model, but in relation to their different aims. However, in the broader philosophic perspective of the aims of education, the education progression model would seem to provide a potentially more liberal or open educational route for young people, although not bearing the hallmarks of obvious or immediate utility for them. It is a salient feature of the whole process that both models require a sufficient supply of jobs in the short and medium term. The education progression model does seem to be a useful, perhaps constructive, means of deferring demand for jobs. Employer-led, job-recruitment model 'new curriculum' organizations largely control the supply and allocation of jobs in the short term. This model is certainly one of substantial advantage to employers, and relates closely to the long sought after reforms of the apprenticeship system.

What is not clear is whether 'new curriculum' organizations

Figure 14.   Job – Recruitment and Education Progression Models of 'New Curriculum' Organizations

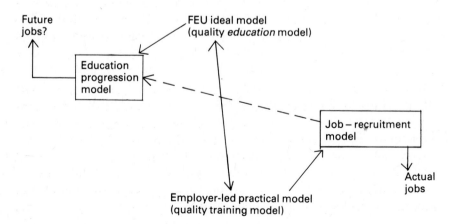

proliferating in terms of one model or the other will be sufficiently dissimilar for them to be typified as different kinds of curriculum organizations. Consequently, it is not feasible, at this stage, to argue whether the YTS will generate *two* 'new curricula', or one. What does seem clear is that YTS will certainly generate at least one 'new curriculum'.

The MSC, using government money, is still laying the pipeline network through which money and 'guidance' can be pumped to fuel and direct the proliferation of 'new curriculum' organizations. Pipelines are being connected to four kinds of areas: private and public sector employers; public sector tertiary education; public sector post-16 secondary education; and possibly, in some form, regressing to 14-16 bottom half public sector secondary education, replacing the present unofficial or informal 'other curriculum'. There is some suggestion, too, that private sector education will become more substantially involved, developing on the present provisions of private companies such as Sight and Sound. At present (March 1983) MSC's emphasis is on employer-led provision of 'new curriculum' organizations. Consequently, the job-recruitment model seems set to dominate initially in scale.

A 'new curriculum' is emerging not only in the English education system, but also as part of the general employment recruitment process in the labour economy. The question of its significance can be taken in three parts: its coverage or scope; its extrinsic worth to trainees and to society at large; its intrinsic worth. It could be argued that an attempt to assess the significance of the 'new curriculum' may be somewhat premature. Admittedly, a degree of speculation is necessarily involved when 'new curriculum' practice is barely under way, particularly if mere assembly of YOP research is deliberately avoided, which it is. However, there is considerable intimation, drawn together in the preceding chapters, about the nature of the 'new curriculum', sufficient to warrant a serious attempt to address the question in the order of its three parts.

In the simplest terms, any curriculum which regulates the experience of half a million or more people per year is bound to be significant. Indeed, even a cursory review of the figures immediately reveals the 'new curriculum' could be, in this sense, the most significant curriculum among curricula for 16–19-year-olds. Taking the government's undertaking to make the 'new curriculum' available to all unemployed minimum age leavers at face value, suggests between 600,000 and 750,000 could take this up. Certainly, the MSC Corporate Plan

1982–1986 (MSC, April 1982) suggested an order of commitment in 1982 comprised of 100,000 in the 'new curriculum' and the remainder in YOP. It was envisaged that by 1983 (September) all these would convert to YTS. It is still not certain that the government through the MSC can deliver a complete conversion of the YOP to the NTI, YTS. The MSC in its corporate plan was hesitant because of its 'lack of resources', and indeed so is every other institution with a finger in the pie. This manoeuvring aside, there is now little doubt that in 1983/84 over half a million young people could be involved. This compares dramatically with 306,000 pupils in schools and 39,000 in FE taking A-levels in 1979/80 (Macfarlane Report, 1980, p. 39, Table 1). So, simply in terms of coverage, the 'new curriculum' would be highly significant if implemented as widely as envisaged by the government.

Its longer-term significance in this respect is to some extent questionable because the catchment for YTS is presently very much linked to the scale of youth unemployment. However, as argued in Chapter 2, there is little prospect of any dramatic fall in these numbers in the next five years. Consequently, if a simple hypothesis is permitted, assuming the YTS in the form of the 'new curriculum' had only a life of five years, then two and a quarter million young people could be affected by it. In broad terms, however, the YTS is unlikely to disappear only through a lack of customers in the medium term. Of course, as intimated in Chapter 3, and argued in Chapter 4, the scheme could disappear for other reasons altogether. These reasons could be generally subsumed under socio-political decisions involving various combinations of power struggle between institutions in or associated with the education system. What is less clear, among such machinations, is whether the 'new curriculum' itself will depend on the scale of youth unemployment and the machinery and resources of the MSC for a continuing existence. Because the curriculum is curiously not the *creation* of government, the MSC or, indeed, any one institutional author, it may not be simply vulnerable to the particular powers of one or other, once it has actually infiltrated the education system and formed as an organizational/institutional behaviour in it. Stopping what has once (finally) started in this system is, perhaps, as difficult as getting it started in the first place. Added to this is the definitive move of the DES to institute a 17+ certificate, which must assuredly associate with the 'new curriculum' in its present YTS form. This seems inevitable in spite of (or perhaps because of) competition between them. The role of government ideology in this is by no means certain; a change of government could have some, but not a decisive, influence on the persistence of the 'new curriculum'. In the widest perspective, then, there is considerable basis upon which to argue that the 'new curriculum' will persist as a significant curriculum in terms of the scope of its human coverage in England and Wales, but that its organizational and institutional forms may shift in the longer term.

The more difficult aspects of an assessment of the significance of the 'new curriculum' are to do with its intrinsic and extrinsic worth. It is not sufficient to suppose a curriculum is significant simply because a large number of people are affected by it; the bubonic plague was significant in such terms. The question of the extrinsic worth of the 'new curriculum' cannot be entirely extricated from that of its intrinsic worth. Nevertheless, something can be made of the distinction between its material value to trainees and to society (extrinsic), and its moral and philosophical status among other curricula (intrinsic). Admittedly there is a certain conceptual difficulty in this distinction in the respect that it can be argued (morally, at least) that a curriculum of little or no intrinsic worth *should* have little or no extrinsic worth; this is to say that the distinction is an artificial one. However, discourse itself tends to the inarticulate under such conceptual and moral precision.

Dealing first with the question of extrinsic worth. This involves, in the first instance, aspects of Chapter 3, but more especially the arguments in Chapter 4 about the certification process and its status. In this central respect there is considerable doubt about the degree to which profile certificates will succeed in the qualifications market. What seems certain is that they will fall into the bottom of the qualifications hierarchy. What is not clear is whether they will prove to have a negative effect for the holders. It is possible that the certificates will provide employers with a means of distinguishing between competing applicants for jobs, and in this respect they may well prove significant, even indispensable to young people in a highly competitive labour market, particularly those who are members of a job-recruitment 'new curriculum' organization. So far as progression to further education and/or training is concerned, the certificates are likely to have significant currency. However, deeply involved in this are the problems associated with the generation of the profiles, in so far as this affects the curriculum process and touches the relations between trainees and teachers, and teachers and evaluators. In consequence there is a distinct possibility that profiles will have difficulty in both facing their *public* purpose and coping with their administrative base, to the extent, perhaps, that they will end up with the cornflakes (mere tokens).

It is possible, therefore, that this most obvious, extrinsic man-ifestation of the 'new curriculum', profile certificates, could end up as negative indicators that the holders belong to the bottom 'class' of school leavers. On the other hand, such certificates could serve as sophisticated labels, distinguishing some leavers as 'better' than others, and more likely to make suitable employees. As YTS training makes virtually no difference to aggregate supply or demand in the labour market itself, then the effect of a 'good' certificate would be significant to the prospects of employment for the particular holder who fell in the 'good' part of this new labelling scheme. In this sense, and in keeping with the arguments of Chapter 2, the effect could be to create a special and new segmentation of what is presently an extensive outer labour market comprised of the present forties and fifties redundant and non-participants or 'failers' in the 'new curriculum', together with those somewhat dubiously referred to as 'the unemployables'.

This leads to a deeper scrutiny of what is meant by extrinsic worth in terms of society at large. The individual may obtain a significant worth from avoiding the 'fail' label which a certification process with effective 'standards' could attach to him – and find it difficult to answer the new question, 'have you got your profile?'. However, is the 'new curriculum' likely to solve two key aspects of the youth unemployment problem? These are usually perceived as: overcoming in the medium term potential structural unemployment at present hidden by the general demand deficiency in the market; and in the short term, to maintain social consensus, which, put simply, means preventing large numbers of disaffected youths forming a permanently alienated group-ing in society, structurally disposed against ever seriously working, and worse, perhaps disposed against 'authority'.

It was argued, especially in Chapter 4, that both depend crucially on the concept of progression. It was found that prospects for progression were seriously deficient, although not entirely nil. Yet, in terms of solving the two key aspects of the youth unemployment problem, the extrinsic worth of the 'new curriculum' is directly proportional to its capacity to progress trainees either to jobs, or to jobs with further education and training, or to further education and training in non-advanced further education (NAFE). Central to the last is the matter of personal allowances. Clearly, too, the preventative effect of the 'new curriculum' upon trainees progressing to HE defined curricula, is a severe and apparently deliberate limitation. Consequent-ly, the capacity of the 'new curriculum' to solve these aspects of the youth unemployment problem is presently as limited as its capacity to enable trainees to progress; this is to say, it cannot significantly contribute to a genuine solution to either aspect of the problem, although something marginally more than a mere cosmetic effect could be hoped for. It must be said, too, that development of the education progression model would defer unemployment for the number and term trainees are progressing through further education courses. This would be in addition to the general deferment of one year's YTS catchment, which is close to the effect of raising the minimum school leaving age to 17.

There remains, therefore, the more general social effect of the 'new curriculum' to consider. Plainly involved is the dramatic extension of 'labelling' to *all* school leavers for the first time. Associated with this is the effective raising of the minimum school leaving age. However, the most striking feature of the 'new curriculum' is its labour market orientation and its determination to direct young people toward a limited range of putative jobs. There is the usual absence of any reference to general studies, except an apparently limited inclusion of schooling in life and personal skills. It is in no sense to be seriously associated with the liberal development of intellectual and aesthetic powers. At present the 'new curriculum' is seen in a context dissociated from education per se, it resides in the remedial, catching-up area of special training courses done largely by FE for a non-educational, quasi-governmental organization (MSC), as an instrument of man-power policy. The perspective that the 'new curriculum' is really to do with training and manpower policy, and not education, could explain the false consensus which surrounds its emergence from the inner recesses of conservative cabinets largely unchallenged by liberal educational opinion. Added to which is the belief by some that the 'new curriculum' is a base upon which better things can be built, given a different political context. However, should the present political context persist, the 'new curriculum' implications are revolutionary, in the precise sense of turning, or returning, the 1980s to the 1880s. The supposed needs of the future labour economy are directly conflated with the educational needs of the individual in a mechanistic and distinctly unimaginative way. Apart from moral or philosophical reservations, there is the troublesome material difficulty that schooling bottom half youngsters for work is not well conceived on either a sufficient manpower analysis, or a *necessary* argument that poetry is less helpful than filing to the future behaviour of the 'vulgar' in a changing society.

However, it is to be presumed that 'they' have already failed poetry, and most else, by the time they leave school at 16 and join a 'new curriculum' organization. As a consequence 'they've had their chance', their opportunity to sample and choose within the liberal secondary school curriculum, and have failed, for some reason or other, to succeed in the traditional examination framework. It is presumed necessary, therefore, to create a new, materially functional, post-16 curriculum aimed at making low ability/attainment youngsters fit to make their way through a working life newly complicated by demands for a literate and numerate and willing-and-able-to-learn new 'labouring' class. In many respects, therefore, the 'new curriculum' may serve apparently important social purposes, but fundamental to this is the not easily grasped nettle that this major curricular provision for the 'other half' has had no affect to date on the overall scheme of things, other than to importantly re-emphasize, by shrewd documentation, the *difference* between the halves of our future. Quite clearly, the struggle to create a common curriculum (see, for example, Lawton, 1975) is made *more* difficult and not less by major unilateral curricular change, oriented to a specifically narrow lower range of occupations and qualifications involving quite categorically the learning of one half only. However, as argued later, the common curriculum to 16 is itself subject to formal differentiation at 14 into a bottom half 'new curriculum', and a top half modernized GCSE curriculum. Consequently, school will divide into secondary technical modern and 'modern' grammar streams in curricular terms, but not in overt institutional terms. Perhaps this will lead to a comprehensive compromise, at long last?

The regression of the 'new curriculum' to pre-16 bottom half pupils negating the liberal concept of a common balanced curriculum for all may be a step backwards. However, minimum age leavers with no paper qualifications literally have nothing at present to show for their years at school, it being the duty of schools to do their best to cram all their pupils into the traditional scheme if they possibly can. That this 'duty' may have been misguided, in the sense that the traditional scheme needed reform, cannot be denied. The advent of the 'new curriculum' does bring a 'common' *alternative* post-16 curriculum, if not a reformed system. Indeed, the advent of the 'new curriculum' does not necessarily in the least *reform* the system. It *could* facilitate reform, but could also enable popular entrenchment of the present quasi-meritocratic status quo. As the latter is more likely, the 'new curriculum' can be treated in isolation, it being separate and alternative to existing secondary school curricula. But, in this particular alone, its moral status can be questioned. In isolation its moral worth can be treated in the utilitarian terms of Mill and Bentham under the principle of greatest happiness or felicity, as grounded upon the *principle of utility*. The fact that it divides society, or, rather, entrenches present division puts the question in the form of the equality of opportunity issue. Here it is worth addressing the distinction made plain in a development (third world) context.

> The point then is whether there is an educational system with proper aims and just means and whether it properly applies to everybody in terms of the evaluation procedures employed as well as their effects. A right to have an equal opportunity for education does not mean a right to be trained to become a member of the elite, exactly because there is no such right. (Shaw, K.E., in Wehnhoerner, 1975, p. 112)

The 'passport' problem is the true heart of the wider issue of equality of opportunity in – through – to education. What is not sufficiently recognized is that the education system is only a contributor (necessary but not sufficient) to the making of passports. In some ways it could be regarded as providing the form which some individuals obtain, but it is the individual's signature which is distinctive, and which is recognized by the establishment/elite as a suitable membership application or not. What is of critical import in the first place is whether the blank form is issued or not to everyone. It is to change both the access to forms and the shape of the form itself that radical educational opinion is sometimes addressed. As already argued, the 'new curriculum' does not seem set to do either, because it provides an alternative *form*, not a replacement. Beyond this it is liable in its operation to act in a newly confirmatory way on the 'other half', effectively containing them in 'their half' – because the 'new curriculum' is preventative of progression (or exchange) between the halves. Profiles are most unlikely to provide the right *form* of passport to the elite; and are, in any case, seriously problematic in themselves.

The question, then, of intrinsic worth cannot be dissociated from the broad socially divisive effect of the 'new curriculum'. But, even if it turns out in such a way, the question still remains whether it is worthwhile in itself. Bentham and Mill have been touched on, yet such a moral philosophy in education can barely extend beyond Spencer's 'What knowledge is most worth?' – which he rightly asked, and seriously debated, but to which he did not supply an answer wholly acceptable then or now. That Mill, Bentham and Spencer should almost automatically seem philosophers relevant to the 'new curriculum' is warning enough of its conservative Victorian liberalism. Which is near to identifying its essential moral paradox (and dilemma): does it serve *only* to school fodder for a capitalist industrial society (the wider interest?), or does it (or can it) serve the individual participant with knowledge in and about that society?

As always, moral dilemmas, and indeed paradoxes, are not new inventions with which to bedevil civil servants and politicians; nor is the question of a curriculum for 'Youth Training'.

> Children should undoubtedly be instructed in such useful acquirements as are *really necessary*. Occupations are divided into liberal and illiberal, and young people should be admitted only to such kinds of knowledge as will prove useful without giving them a 'working class' (vulgar) outlook – an outlook which is bred by those occupations, arts and sciences which unfit the body, soul, or mind of a freeman for the pursuit and practice of virtue. The 'working class' (vulgar) mentality may accordingly be said to arise from any art or craft which tends to undermine physical fitness (deteriorate the condition of the body), as well as any employment which is undertaken solely for gain and therefore absorbs and impoverishes the mind. There are also some liberal studies to which a freeman may devote himself *only up to a certain point*; if he goes too far, hoping to reach perfection, the same disastrous consequences will ensue. Much, however, depends upon the object with which a man sets to work. If he does so for his own needs, to help his friends, or with a view to goodness, his action will not be regarded illiberal; but the same work repeatedly undertaken in obedience to others must be set down as menial and servile. (Aristotle, *Politics*, Book VIII; parenthetics provide alternative translation in Loeb Library Edition)

This is, perhaps, a somewhat peripatetic way of noting a certain 'vulgarity' about the 'new curriculum'.

Finally, it is necessary to recognize that the 'new curriculum' *is* susceptible to liberalization in the future, and it is possible for it to serve the 16–19 age group as one *choice* in a full range of curricula. This will depend entirely on the nature of both the 'problem' of youth unemployment and the policy of government. At present unemployment is seen as an illiberal art (or craft) which requires illiberal medication and special statistical treatment in the hope that 'they' will become addicted to the cure. In the final analysis, young people will take their medicine to be sure, but for the course of treatment to succeed their experience of the first dose should not be too bitter. Nor should it be intractably supposed by the scheme of things in which the 'new curriculum' resides, that the 'halves' are somehow a proper, or even real, division. Jude may be long dead, but his ghost could haunt the 'new curriculum'

> It was not till now, when he found himself actually on the Spot of his enthusiasm, that Jude perceived how far away from the object of that enthusiasm he really was. Only a wall divided him from those happy young contempories of his with whom he shared a common mental life; men who had nothing to do from morning til night but to read, mark, learn, and inwardly digest. Only a wall ... but what a wall. (Hardy, 1972 ed., p. 92)

And, talking of 'Walls', if the 'dimmest' youngster is able to put two bricks together and discover:

> We don't need no education
> We don't need no thought control
> No dark sarcasm in the classroom
> Teacher leave us kids alone
> All in all it's just another brick in the wall
> All in all you're just another brick in the wall. (Pink Floyd, 1979, 5th track)

what next?

Well, there is, at present, a developing interrelationship between MSC and DES initiatives directed 'in cabinet' by a small circle of ministers around the Prime Minister. Although the specific grant for LEA provided education was defeated recently (Walker, 1983, pp. 25–8), centralizing direct control of education and training is progressing firmly. DES school curriculum and new examination proposals, the specific directing grant through MSC, particularly the New Training and Vocational Education Initiative (NTVEI), are not ad hoc or accidental developments, but part of a conservative policy framework for education and training evolved and acted on at cabinet level. The reshaping of craft and technician apprentice training, disassembly of industrial training boards, possible privatization of skill centres and encouragement of private training companies, the emergence of an adult retraining strategy, are all interrelated actions to achieve broad conservative education and training policy objectives.

The National Advisory Board for Public Sector Further and Higher Education (NAB) and, in the wider, but related perspective, university funding, represent the commitment of the Conservative Party to '... review the relationship between school, further education and training to see how better use can be made of existing resources' (*Conservative Party Manifesto*, 1979, p. 25).

The underlying aim of Conservative policy is to modernize educational and training curricula to generate a killed and adaptable future labour force in a free market economy. This means orienting the secondary school curriculum toward technological and scientific education closely connected to industry and industry's perceptions of its needs. The operation of a liberal, common, balanced (comprehensive) curriculum in secondary schools is seen as an ineffective and expensive way to meet these objectives. Balancing the needs (and desires) of the individual against the needs of the economy in the liberal tradition of the education service obstructs the achievement of Conservative objectives. Consequently, the balance is to be tipped toward the 'greater good': the economy and a free market meritocracy. This means producing workers who will fit into such an economy. The education service, stimulated by alternative competing agencies (interorganizational competition), together with competition within the service (intraorganizational competition) must produce workers to fit the spectrum of labour demand in a putative 'new economy'. Some (goats) must be clever, and educated to advanced levels of cognitive skills, preferably highly related to science and technology, others will need to service these workers and fit in at lesser levels. Low attainment school children (sheep) 'obviously' fit into the lesser levels and need schooling to them. The present secondary school curriculum does not particularly cope with or provide for these youngsters. The informal 'other curriculum' needs formalizing and working out in vocational terms, that is, training for work at lesser levels in the 'new economy'. This 'new curriculum' should be geared to the 'new economy', and should emerge as an alternative curriculum for the less bright (the bottom half). At the moment national manpower analysis does not reveal, with any confidence, whether these youngsters should be trained for 'fish-grabbing' or 'horse-clubbing', but it is clear that they ought to be at the least schooled for work at lesser levels in the 'new economy'.

Great economic advantage is expected to flow from such longer-term structural change in the secondary school curriculum. In the immediate term the 'new curriculum' is being fed into the system from the 'top', as it were. In other words, the YTS is expensively geared to the immediate problem of massive and politically dangerous youth unemployment. Its manpower policy logic is flawed, but not irretrievably. However, its immediate and continuing removal of very large numbers of young unemployed from the register is attractive to all politicians, whatever their persuasion. The relationship between a falling school population (and leavers), a pick-up in general demand, a unified GCSE, for the bright, a 17+ pre-vocational leaving certificate for the bottom half, NTVEI, reformed apprenticeships, expensive personal YTS allowances, will ensure 'new curriculum' organizations at present operating for minimum age school leavers and 17-year-old unemployeds could naturally and easily regress into the secondary school system for pre-16 bottom halfers. This would ultimately leave a residuum of 17 (16)+ leavers 'failing' in the job market. These could be mopped up and mostly made employable by a special MSC scheme, perhaps evolving from a present 'disadvantaged' scheme. This all seems to work out rather tidily. Selection or 'streaming' can be re-established as a legitimate activity, perhaps not at 11+, but at 13+. The 'new curriculum' seems a neat fit.

> ... by creating new courses in 'low status' knowledge areas, and restricting their availability to those who have already 'failed' in terms of academic definitions of knowledge, these failures are seen as individual failures, either of motivation, ability or circumstances, and not failures of the academic system itself. These courses, which explicitly deny pupils access to kinds of knowledge which are associated with rewards, prestige and power in our society are thus given a kind of legitimacy, which masks the fact that educational success in terms of them would still be defined as 'failure'. (Young, 1971, p. 40)

Bibliography

ARGLES, M. (1964) *South Kensington to Robbins*, London, Longmans.

ARISTOTLE, *Politics*, Trans. and ed. by J. Warrington, Heron Books.

ASSOCIATION OF COLLEGES IN FURTHER AND HIGHER EDUCATION (7 June 1982) *Report of the Youth Task Group*, paper to ACFHE Seminar held in Bath, 10 June 1982.

AVIS, J. (1983) 'ABC and the new vocational consensus', in *Journal of Further and Higher Education*, 7, 1, spring.

AVON LEA, FE Sub-Committee (30 March 1982) *Report of the Director of Education: Avon Youth Training Scheme*, County of Avon/LEA.

AVON TEACHERS' CONSULTATIVE COMMITTEE (March 1975) *Sixteen to Nineteen*, ATCC.

BATH TECHNICAL COLLEGE (1981) *Development Plan 1980/1–1985/6*, Governors Bath Technical College.

BATH TECHNICAL COLLEGE (1975) *Wider Opportunities in a Rational System: The Development of 16–19 Education*, Bath Technical College Academic Board.

BECHER, T. *et al.* (1981) *Policies for Educational Accountability*, London, Heinemann.

BECHER, T. and MACLURE, S. (1978) *Accountability in Education*, Social Science Research Council, Educational Research Board, NFER.

BELL, R. (Ed.) (1973) *Education in Great Britain and Ireland*, Open University Press.

BENJAMIN, H. (1939) 'The saber-tooth curriculum', in Hooper (1971) pp. 7–15.

BERNBAUM, G. (1977) *Knowledge and Ideology in the Sociology of Education*, London, Macmillan.

BERNSTEIN, B. (1971) 'On the classification and framing of educational knowledge', in YOUNG (1971) pp. 19–69.

BISHOP, A.S. (1971) *The Rise of a Central Authority for English Education*, Cambridge, Cambridge University Press.

BLACK, H.D. and DOCKRELL, W.B. (1980), 'Assessment in the affective domain: Do we, can we, should we?', in *British Educational Research Journal*, 6, 2.

BLOOM, B.S. (Ed.) (1956) *Taxonomy of Educational Objectives*, Vols. I and II,

London, Longman.

BLUM, A. (1971) 'The corpus of knowledge as a normative order', in YOUNG (1971).

BRITISH PRINTING INDUSTRIES FEDERATION (BPIF) (28 January 1983) *New BPIF/NGA Training Agreement*, circular.

BROADFOOT, P. (1980) 'The Scottish pupil profile system', in BURGESS and ADAMS (1980) *Outcomes of Education*, Macmillan Education, pp. 56 ff.

BRUNER, J.S. (1966a) *Toward a Theory of Instruction*, Harvard, Mass., Harvard University Press, 4th ed.

BRUNER, J.S. (1966b). *The Process of Education*, Harvard, Mass., Harvard University Press.

BUTCHER, H.J. (1968) *Human Intelligence: Its Nature and Assessment*, London, Methuen.

CANTOR, L.M. and ROBERTS, I.F. (1979) *Further Education Today: A Critical Review*, London, Routledge and Kegan Paul.

CONSERVATIVE PARTY MANIFESTO (1979) Conservative Central Office.

COOPER, K. (1976) 'Curriculum evaluation – definition and boundaries', in TAWNEY (1976).

COSIN, B.R. (1972) *Education: Structure and Society*, OUP and Penguin.

COTTERELL, A.B. and HELEY, E.W. (Eds) (1980) *Tertiary: A Radical Approach to Post-Compulsory Education*, Stanley Thornes.

CURTIS, S.J. (1948) *History of Education in Great Britain*, University Tutorial Press.

DAVIES, I.K. (1976) *Objectives in Curriculum Design*, McGraw-Hill.

DEAN, J. (1980) 'Alternatives to the traditional sixth form', in *Coombe Lodge Report*, 13, 9, p. 400.

DENT, H.C. (1944) *The Education Act 1944*, London, University of London Press Limited.

DENT, H.C. (1977) *Education in England and Wales*, Hodder and Stoughton.

DES (DEPARTMENT OF EDUCATION AND SCIENCE) (12 July 1965) *The Organisation of Secondary Education*, Circular 10/65, London.

DES (30 June 1970) *The Organisation of Secondary Education*, Circular 10/70, London.

DES (1977) *The Educational System of England and Wales*, new ed., London.

DES (April 1979a) *A Better Start in Working Life: A Consultative Paper*, London.

DES (April 1979b) *Providing Educational Opportunities for 16–18 Year Olds*, A Consultative Paper, London.

DES (Oct. 1980) *Examinations 16–18: A Consultative Paper*, London.

DES (Jan. 1981), *Education for 16–19 Year Olds*, London.

DES (May 1982) 'Pupil and school leavers: Future numbers', in *Report on Education*, No. 97.

DES/WELSH OFFICE (March 1981) *The School Curriculum*, London, HMSO.

DES/WELSH OFFICE (May 1982) *17+: A New Qualification*, London, HMSO.

DES/WELSH OFFICE (Nov. 1982) *Examinations at 16-Plus: A Statement of Policy*, London, HMSO.

DEPARTMENT OF EMPLOYMENT (Dec. 1981), *A New Training Initiative: A Programme for Action*, Cmnd. 8455, London, HMSO.

EAGLESHAM, E.J.R. (1956) *From School Board to Local Authority*, London,

Routledge and Kegan Paul.

EAGLESHAM, E.J.R. (1967) *The Foundations of Twentieth-Century Education in England*, London, Routledge and Kegan Paul.

EBBUTT, K. and BROWN, R. (1978) 'The structure of power in the F.E. College', in *Journal of Further and Higher Education*, 2, 3, autumn.

EDWARDS, T.A. (1982) *The Sixteen to Nineteen Jungle: Can Bath Technical College Clear a Path for the New Training Initiative?* unpublished.

EGGLESTON, J. (1977) *The Sociology of the School Curriculum*, London, Routledge and Kegan Paul.

ENGELS, (1892) *The Condition of the Working-Class in England in 1844*, George Allen and Unwin.

ETZIONI, A. (1961) *A Comprarative Analysis of Complex Organisations*, Glenco, Ill., Free Press.

FARLEY, M. (Feb. 1982) (Assistant Secretary, National Association of Teachers in Further and Higher Education), 'The NTI: A positive agenda – a foolish White Paper', in *NATFHE Journal*, February, pp. 11–13.

FENWICK, K. and McBRIDE, P. (1981) *The Government of Education*, Oxford, Martin Robertson.

FEU (FURTHER EDUCATION CURRICULUM REVIEW AND DEVELOPMENT UNIT) (June 1979) *A Basis for Choice: Report of a Study Group on Post 16 Pre-Employment Courses*, London.

FEU (Jan. 1981a) *Signposts: A Map of 16–19 Educational Provision*, London.

FEU (Jan. 1981b) *Vocational Preparation*, London.

FEU (March 1981), *Curriculum Control: A Review of Major Styles of Curriculum Design in F.E.*, PR 8, vol. 1, London.

FEU (July 1981) *Annual Report 1980–81*, London.

FEU (Sept. 1981) *ABC in Action: A Report from an FEU/CGLI Working Party on the Piloting of 'A Basis for Choice'*, 1979–81, London.

FEU (Dec. 1981) *Progressing from Vocational Preparation: A Discussion of Issues*, London.

FEU (June 1982) *Teaching Skills: Towards a Strategy of Staff Development and Support for Vocational Preparation*, London.

FEU (Aug. 1982) *Promoting Curriculum Innovation*, London.

FEU (Sept. 1982) *Profiles: A Review of Issues and Practice in the Use and Development of Student Profiles*, London.

FEU (Nov. 1982) *Basic Skills*, London.

FLOUD, J., HALSEY, A.H. and MARTIN, F.M. (1957) *Social Class and Educational Opportunity*, London, Heinemann.

FOWLER, G. (Ed.) (1973) *Decision Making in British Education*, Open University Press.

GOLBY, M. *et al.* (1975) *Curriculum Design*, Open University Press.

GOODLAD, J.I. *et al.* (1979) *Curriculum Inquiry*, McGraw-Hill.

GRAY, H.L. (1975) 'Exchange and conflict in the school', in HOUGHTON, V. (Ed.) *Management in Education*, Vol. I, Oxford, Oxford University Press, pp.253–65.

GREEN, M. (1971) 'Curriculum and consciousness', in BECK, J. (Ed.) *Worlds Apart*,

HANDY. C.B. (1976) *Understanding Organisations*, Harmondsworth, Penguin.

HARDY, T. *Jude the Obscure,* started by Hardy in 1887, first published 1895, this edition 1972, London, Macmillan.

HASLEGRAVE, H.L. (1969) *Haslegrave Report,* London, HMSO.

HERZBERG, F., MAUSNER, B. and SNYDERMAN, B. (1959) *The Motivation to Work,* 2nd ed., New York, Wiley.

HILL, A. (1977) *Accountability and Evaluation in the Junior High School,* MEd dissertation, University of Bath, Library.

HIRST, P. (1969) 'The logic of the curriculum'. in *Journal of Curriculum Studies,* 1, 2, pp. 142–58.

HIRST, P. 'Liberal education and the nature of knowledge', in ARCHAMBAULT R. *Philosophical Analyses and Education,*

HIRST, P. and PETERS, R.S. (1970) *The Logic of Education,* London, Routledge and Kegan Paul.

HMI (Her Majesty's Inspectors of Schools) (Dec. 1979) *Aspects of Secondary Education in England: A Survey by HM Inspectors of Schools,* London, HMSO.

HOLLY, D. (1973) *Beyond Curriculum,* Hart-Davis, MacGibbon.

HOOPER, R. (Ed.) (1971) *The Curriculum: Context, Design and Development,* Open University Press.

HORN, C.A. and P.L.R. (1981) 'Payment by results and technical instruction', in *Journal of Further and Higher Education,* 5, 1, Spring, pp. 30–9.

HORTON, (1981) 'Macfarlane in context', in *Coombe Lodge Report,* 14, 6, pp. 339 ff.

HUGHES, J.L. (1975) 'How should we measure unemployment?', in *British Journal of Industrial Relations,* 13, 3, November, pp. 317–33.

HURT, J.S. (1979) *Elementary Schooling and the Working Classes 1860–1918,* London, Routledge and Kegan Paul.

IMS (INSTITUTE OF MANPOWER STUDIES) (1981) *London into Work Development Project: Job Opportunities for Young People,* Brighton.

IMS (Feb. 1982) *Foundation Training Issues: A Report for the Manpower Services Commission,* Brighton.

JENNINGS, R.E. (1977) *Education and Politics: Policy-Making in Local Education Authorities,* Batsford.

JOHNSON, R. (1970) 'Educational policy and social control in early Victorian England'. in *Past and Present,* November.

JOHNSON, R. (1979) *Working Class Culture,* Hutchinson, esp. ch. 3.

JOSEPH, K. (Sir) (Sept. 1974) Preston Speech, *The Times,* 6 September 1974 (in HUGHES, 1975, p. 332).

KATZ, D. (1964) 'The motivational basis of organisational behaviour', in *Behavioural Science.*

KERR, C. (1954) 'The Balkanisation of labor markets', in *Labor Mobility and Economic Opportunity,* MIT Press, New York, Wiley.

KEYNES, J.M. (1936) *The General Theory of Employment, Interest and Money,* London, Macmillan.

KING, R. (1976) *School and College: Studies of Post-Sixteen Education,* London, Routledge and Kegan Paul.

LAWLER, E.E. and PORTER, L.W. (1976) 'Antecedent attitudes of effective managerial performance', in *Organisational Behaviour and Human Perform-*

ance, Vol. 2, pp. 122–42.

LAWTON, D. (1975) *Class Culture and the Curriculum*, London, Routledge and Kegan Paul.

LAWTON, D. (1980) *The Politics of the School Curriculum*, London, Routledge and Kegan Paul.

LE-GRAND, JULIAN (1982) *The Strategy of Equality*, London, George Allen and Unwin.

LITT, E. and PARKINSON, M.P. (1979) *U.S. and U.K. Educational Policy: A Decade of Reform*, Praeger.

MCCLELLAND, D.C., ATKINSON, J.W., CLARK, R.A., and LOWELL, E.L. (1953), *The Achievement Motive*, New York, Appleton Century Crofts.

MACDONALD-ROSS, M. (1973) 'Behavioural objectives: A critical review', in GOLBY *et al.* (1975).

MACFARLANE, E. (1978) *Sixth Form Colleges*, London, Heinemann.

MACFARLANE, N. (Dec. 1980) *Macfarlane Report: Education for 16–19 Year Olds: A Review Undertaken for the Government and the Local Authority Associations*, London, HMSO.

MACLURE, J. STUART, (1965) *Educational Documents England and Wales 1816 to the Present Day*, Methuen.

MACLURE, S. (1978) 'Background to the accountability debate', in BECHER and MACLURE (1978).

MAGER, R.F. (1975) *Preparing Instructional Objectives*, 2nd ed., Fearon, Pitman.

MARKELL, G. (1982) in REES, T.L. and ATKINSON, P. *Youth Unemployment and State Intervention*, Routledge Direct Editions.

MASLOW, A. (1954) *Motivation and Personality*, HARPER and ROW.

MIDDLETON, N. and WEITZMAN, S. (1976) *A Place for Everyone*, Gollancz.

MILL, J.S. (1962) *Utilitarianism*, Ed. by M. WARNOCK, Fontana Library.

MITCHELL, T.R. and BIGLAN, A. (1971) 'Instrumentality theories: Current uses in psychology', in *Psychological Bulletin*, 76, pp. 432–54.

MSC (Manpower Services Commission) (Oct. 1976) *Towards a Comprehensive Manpower Policy*, London.

MSC (May 1977) *Young People and Work*, London.

MSC (1978? undated), *Training for (Vital) Skills: A Programme for Action*, London.

MSC (1978) *Making Experience Work: Principles and Guidelines for Providing Work Experience*, London.

MSC (May 1980) *Manpower Review 1980*, London.

MSC (1981) *Annual Report 1980–81*, London.

MSC (March 1981) *MSC Corporate Plan 1981–85*, London.

MSC (May 1981a) *A New Training Initiative: A Consultative Document*, London.

MSC (May 1981b) *The Youth Opportunities Programme and the Local Education Authority*, London.

MSC (July 1981) *A Framework for the Future: A Sector by Sector Review of Industrial and Commercial Training*, London.

MSC (Nov. 1981) *Trainee Centred Reviewing* (TCR), Research and Development Series, No. 2, London.

MSC (Dec. 1981a) *A New Training Initiative: An Agenda for Action*, London.

MSC (Dec. 1981b) *Trainees Come First: The Organisational Structure of Community Project YOP Schemes*, Research and Development Series, No. 4, London.

MSC (1982) *Manpower Review 1981*, London.

MSC (April 1982a) *The Benefit of Experience*, Research and Development Series, No. 5, London.

MSC (April 1982b) *Corporate Plan, 1982–86*, London.

MSC (April 1982c) *Youth Task Group Report*, London.

MSC (Aug. 1982) *Learning at Work: The Tavistock Guide*, Research and Development Series, No. 9, London.

MSC/FEU (Sept. 1982) *A New Training Initiative: Joint Statement by MSC/FEU*, London.

MSC (Jan. 1983) *Youth Training News*, Issue No. 1.

MUKHERJEE, S. (1974) *There's Work to Be Done: Unemployment and Manpower Policies*, London, HMSO.

MUNGHAM, G (1982) 'Workless youth as moral panic', in REES, T.L. and ATKINSON, P. (Eds), *Youth Unemployment and State Intervention*, London, Routledge Kegan Paul.

NATFHE (National Association of Teachers in Further and Higher Education) (1979) *Education and Training for the 16–19's: A Discussion Paper*, London.

NATFHE (1980) *College Administration: A Handbook*, London.

NATFHE (29 March 1982) *A New Training Initiative: A Checklist*, Education Department Circular 19/82.

NATFHE (March 1982) *Vocational Preparation for the Young Employed*, London, Manpower Services Commission.

NATFHE (June 1982) *The Youth Opportunities Programme: The Contribution of Further Education*, London, Manpower Services Commission.

NEWELL, R. (1982) 'Rise of the MSC', in *NATFHE Journal*, November.

NEWSOM REPORT (1963) *Half Our Future*, report of the Minister of Education's Central Advisory Council, London, HMSO.

NJCTFE (National Joint Council for Teachers in Further Education) (1981) *Scheme of Conditions of Service*, NJCTFE.

OECD (Organization for Economic Co-operation and Development) (1975) *Reviews of National Policies for Education: Education Development Strategy in England and Wales*, Paris.

OECD (Centre for Educational Research, CERI) (1972) *Styles of Curriculum Development*, Paris.

ORLOSKY, D. and SMITH, B. (1978) *Curriculum Development: Issues and Insights*, Chicago, Ill., Rand McNally.

PACKWOOD, T. and TURNER, C. (1977) 'Hierarchy, anarchy and accountability: Contrasting perspectives', in (BEMAS) *Educational Management and Administration*, 5, 2, Spring, pp. 1–12.

PAISEY, A. (1982) 'Participation in school organization', in *Education Management and Administration*, 10. 1, February.

PETERSON, A.D.C. (1972) *The International Baccalaureate: An Experiment in International Education*, Harrap.

PINK FLOYD (1979) *The Wall*, CBS.

POLLARD, A. (undated), 'O and A level: Keeping up the standards', in COX, C.B. and DYSON, A.E. (Eds) *Black Paper Two: The Crisis in Education*, The Critical Quarterly Society.

POPHAM, W.J. (1975) *Educational Evaluation*, Prentice-Hall.

PORTER, L.W. and LAWLER, E.E. (1968) *Managerial Attitudes and Performance*, Homewook I.U., Irwin-Dorsey.

RENAUD, G. (1974) *Experimental Period of the International Baccalaureate: Objectives and Results*, Paris, Unesco Press, International Bureau of Education.

RICHMOND, W.K. (1968) *Readings in Education*, Methuen.

RIPA (1981) *Government Policy Initiatives 1979–80: Some Case Studies in Public Administration,* Ed. by P.M. JACKSON, London.

ROGERS, R. (1980) *Crowther to Warnock*, London, Heinemann Educational Books.

ROUSSEAU J.-J. (1762) *Rousseau's Emile or Treatise on Education*, 1983 ed trans. by W.H. PAYNE, London, Arnold.

RUSSELL, B. (1912) *The Problems of Philosophy*, 1967 ed., Oxford, Oxford Paperbacks.

SARAN, R. (1982) 'The politics of bargaining relationships during Burnham negotiations', in *Educational Management and Administration*, 10, June, pp. 173–7.

SCHEIN, E.H. (1970) *Organizational Psychology*, 2nd ed., Prentice-Hall.

SCHOOLS COUNCIL (1969) *General Studies 16–18*, Working Paper No. 25, London.

SCHOOLS COUNCIL (1971) *Choosing a Curriculum for the Young School Leaver*, Working Paper No. 33, Evans/Methuen Educational.

SCHOOLS COUNCIL (1972) *16–17: Growth and Response, 1. Curricular Bases*, Working Paper No. 45, Evans/Methuen Educational.

SCHOOLS COUNCIL (1973) *16–19: Growth and Response 2. Examination Structure*, Working Paper No. 46, Evans/Methuen Educational.

SCHOOLS COUNCIL (1978) *Examinations at 18+: The N. and F. Studies*, Working Paper No. 60, Evans/Methuen Educational.

SCHOOLS COUNCIL (1981) *The Practical Curriculum*, Working Paper No. 70, Methuen Educational.

SCOTTISH VOCATIONAL PREPARATION UNIT (SVPU) (Feb. 1982) *Assessment in Youth Training: Made to Measure?*

SCRACFE (Standing Conference of Regional Advisory Councils for Further Education) (Oct. 1980) *Foundations for Working Life: Report of a Working Party on the Education and Training of the 16–19 Age Group.*

Shorter Oxford English Dictionary (1956) 3rd ed., rev., Oxford.

SIMON, B. (1972) *The Radical Tradition in Education in Britain*, London, Lawrence and Wishart.

SIMON, B (1974) *The Two Nations and the Educational Structure 1780–1870*, London, Lawrence and Wishart.

SIMON, B. (1974) *Education and the Labour Movement 1870–1920*, London, Lawrence and Wishart.

SMALL, N. (1983) 'Adults, the NTI and education', in *Educational Management and Administration*, 11, 1, February.

SOCKETT, H. (Ed.) (1980) *Accountability in the English Educational System*,

Unibooks/Hodder and Stoughton.

SPENCER, H. (1929) *Education: Intellectual, Moral and Physical,* Thinkerd Library edition.

STUFFLEBEAM, D.S. (1974) 'Alternative approaches to education evaluation', in *Evaluation in Education: Current Applications,* McCutchan Publishing.

TAWNEY, D. (Ed.) (1976) *Curriculum Evaluation Today: Trends and Implications,* Schools Research Council.

TAYLOR, P.H., REID, W.A. and HOLLEY, B.J. (1974) *The English Sixth Form: A Case Study in Curriculum Research,* London, Routledge and Kegan Paul.

TAYLOR REPORT (1977), *A New Partnership for our Schools,* London, HMSO, for DES/Welsh Office.

THOMAS, R.E. (1982) 'Personal opinion: New Training Initiative', in *Training,* 7, 11, February, pp. 8–9.

THOMPSON, E.P. (1963) *The Making of the English Working Class,* Gollancz.

TIBBLE, J.W. (Ed.) (1970) *The Extra Year,* London, Routledge and Kegan Paul. *Times Educational Supplement, The* (4 March, 1983) editorial.

VROOM, V.H. (1964) *Work and Motivation,* New York, Wiley.

WALKER, D. (1983) 'Department of Education and Local Authorities: Breaking the partnership in order to survive', in *Public Money,* 2, 4, March.

WEBER, M. (1948 trans) *From Max Weber: Essays in Sociology,* Trans. by H.H. GERTH and C. WRIGHT MILLS London, Routledge & Kegan Paul.

WEHNHOERNER, A. (1975) *Elites and Development,* Regional Experts Workshop in Bangkok, organized by Freidrich-Ebert-Stiftung, Federal Republic of Germany, 12–18 May 1975.

WHITE, J. (6 March 1969) 'The curriculum mongers: Education in reverse', in HOOPER (1971), pp. 279–80.

WHITE, J. (1974) 'Curriculum by statute', in *The Times Educational Supplement,* 31 May.

WHITE, J.P. (1971) 'Curriculum Evaluation', in GOLBY *et al.* (1975).

WILLIAMS, R. (1958a) *Culture and Society 1780–1950* Relican.

WILLIAMS, R. (1958b) *The Long Revolution,* Extracts in Pelican Books (1965) pp. 61, 161–8, and HOOPER (1971) pp. 42ff.

WILLIAMSON, H. (1982), in REES, T.L. and ATKINSON P. *Youth Unemployment and State Interventions,* Routledge Direct Editions.

WINTER, R. (1976) 'Keeping files: Aspects of bureaucracy and education', in YOUNG and WHITTY (1976).

YOUNG, M.F.D. (1971) *Knowledge and Control, New Directions for the Sociology of Education,* Collier Macmillan.

YOUNG, M.F.D. and WHITTY, G. (1976) *Explorations in the Politics of School Knowledge,* Driffield, Nafferton Books.

YOUNG, M.F.D. and WHITTY, G. (1977), *Society, State and Schooling,* Lewes, The Falmer Press.

Author Index

Subject Index

allowances, 110–13
assessment, 75–100
Assessment of Performance Unit (APU), 53
Association of Colleges in Further and Higher Education (ACFHE), 54

'Balkanization'
of labour markets, 28
Britain, *passim*
Business Education Council (BEC), 36, 99, 140, 141–3

Callaghan, J., 37
Cambridge Economic Policy Group (CEPG), 31
Certificate in Pre-Vocational Education (CPVE), 40, 116–17
Certificate of Secondary Education (CSE), 46, 54, 91, 95, 104–6, 110, 113–14, 115, 117, 143, 144
City and Guilds of London Institute (CGLI), 54, 64, 140, 141–3
Community Industry Programme, 23
Construction Industry Training Board (CITB), 87
curriculum, *passim*
definition of, 1–17
and progression, 101–45

Department of Education and Science (DES), 41–2, 45, 48, 53, 59, 99, 111, 115, 144, 156, 163
see also entry in Author Index

education progression model, 137–45, 152–4
employment, 1–2, 19–48, 49–100, 102–3, 149–50

Further Education Curriculum Review and Development Unit (FEU), 14–15, 34, 36, 46, 48, 54, 61–76, 83–6, 88–9, 95, 97–8, 100, 102, 104, 105, 106, 109, 112, 116–18, 125, 139–41, 150–4
see also entry in Author Index
Further Education Staff College (Coombe Lodge), 54

General Certificate of Education (GCE), 12–13, 54, 95, 104–5, 115, 117, 143, 144
General Certificate of Secondary Education (GCSE), 116–17, 120, 160, 165
Great Debate, 37

Her Majesty's Inspectorate (HMI), 53
see also entry in Author Index

Industrial Research Training Unit (IRTU), 90